The Voice of Mother Earth

Then Spirit Walker spoke:

When I was a boy, I was taken to the base of the mountain by a very old wise man. Although most of us were only part Indian, we were still accepted as their own by the full-blooded members of the tribe. We lived with the white people in the area, but often kept our heritage and ideas to ourselves. The old wise man was a medicine man and there were three of us, but only one would be selected that day to take his place. I don't remember the year exactly, but it must have been around 1910. He took us to the base of the mountain and showed us the chamber and the stones that were behind it. He told us that a long time ago no one was allowed past the point of the chamber unless you were a sachem or a powerful medicine man. He said that although the spirits are still present they are much weaker than they were centuries ago.

He then took us over to one of the great stones that was standing up and asked us to put our hands on it and place our ear against it one at a time. With each boy he asked, "What do you hear?" The first boy said nothing, then I tried and he asked once again, "What do you hear?" I then heard a humming sound that almost sounded like a musical instrument; it pulsated. I then took my hands off the rock, and it stopped. I told him what I heard and he smiled and said, "You are gifted, you are chosen for you can hear Mother Earth sing." The other boy then ran to the stone and tried to listen, but he heard nothing. He then dismissed the other two and sent them home. The wise man then sat me down and began to tell me the story about the stones and the people who put them there.

Spirit Walker then grew tired and told Phil that he would continue the story the next day. Phil retired to his room and contemplated what he had been told that day. What did he mean by "Mother Earth singing?" As Phil thought about it more deeply he realized that he had seen the stones that Spirit Walker was talking about . . .

About the Authors

Philip Imbrogno is a respected science educator whose research has been documented in *Unsolved Mysteries, Sightings, American Undercover,* and *Encounters.* Marianne Horrigan is a paranormal researcher who has had articles published in *Fate* and *UFO Universe.*

To Write to the Authors

If you wish to contact the authors or would like more information about this book, please write to the author in care of Llewellyn Worldwide and we will forward your request. Both the authors and publisher appreciate hearing from you and learning of your enjoyment of this book and how it has helped you. Llewellyn Worldwide cannot guarantee that every letter written to the authors can be answered, but all will be forwarded. Please write to:

Philip Imbrogno and Marianne Horrigan
c/o Llewellyn Worldwide
P.O. Box 64383, Dept. K357-3
St. Paul, MN 55164-0383, U.S.A.

Please enclose a self-addressed stamped envelope for reply, or $1.00 to cover costs. If outside U.S.A., enclose international postal reply coupon.

CELTIC MYSTERIES IN NEW ENGLAND

Celtic Mysteries in New England

Philip Imbrogno & Marianne Horrigan

2000
Llewellyn Publications
St. Paul, Minnesota 55164-0383
U.S.A.

FIRST EDITION
First Printing, 2000

Cover design: Lisa Novak
Cover photo and interior photos: Philip Imbrogno
Book design: Michael Maupin

Library of Congress Cataloging-in-Publication Data

Imbrogno, Philip J.
  Celtic mysteries in New England / Philip J. Imbrogno & Marianne Horrigan.
    p. cm.
  Includes index.
  ISBN 1-56718-357-3
  1. Druids and druidism. 2. Human-alien encounters—New England.
  3. Unidentified flying objects—Sightings and encounters—New England.
  4. Megalithic monuments—New England. 5. Civilization, Celtic—
  Miscellanea. I. Horrigan, Marianne. II. Title.

  BF2050 I435 2000
  001.94—dc21   99-058548

Llewellyn Publications
A Division of Llewellyn Worldwide, Ltd.
P.O. Box 64383, Dept. K357-3
St. Paul, MN 55164-0383, U.S.A.
www.llewellyn.com

Other Books by Philip Imbrogno

with Marianne Horrigan
Contact of the 5th Kind

with J. Allen Hynek and Bob Pratt
Night Siege: The Hudson Valley UFO Sightings

Acknowledgments

We wish to thank the following individuals and organizations: Martin Brech, David Barron, Jack Allen Horrigan, Rochelle Colette Bussi, Loretta and Scott Chaney, Karen Williams, Rich Zygmunt, Darlene Bruns, Mark and Lena, Charles Boyle, The Gungywamp Society, NEARA, Norwalk Archeological Society, and the Putnam County Historical Society.

For William,
who will always be in my heart.

Contents

CHAPTER 1

Lost in Time

*T*HE COUNTIES OF PUTNAM and Westchester are located in the beautiful Hudson Valley of New York. Despite their close proximity to New York City and their high population, the area conceals some of the greatest mysteries in North America. It is here in the small town of Sleepy Hollow that Washington Irving's tale of the Headless Horseman was born. This area also contains many American Indian legends of magical and sacred places, which they believed were gateways to another world. The descendants of these Native Americans today still tell their grandchildren tales, where wonders can be seen, where earth spirits dwell.

It was also in the Hudson Valley that one of the most perplexing series of UFO sightings took place. From 1983 until 1995, thousands of people had an incredible sighting of a giant boomerang-shaped object with multicolored lights (see color Plate 2). The object was reported to have been the size of several football fields, and was witnessed by many people from all walks of life. These sightings are documented in two books, *Night Siege: The Hudson Valley UFO Sightings,* and *Contact of the Fifth Kind.* Our research into these series of UFO sightings and UFO-related events led us to a greater mystery, a mystery that may have begun over 3,000 years ago.

Early into our research, while investigating the multitude of paranormal events in the southern New York area, we became aware of a number of mysterious stone chambers and carved monoliths scattered throughout New York, Connecticut, Massachusetts, and Vermont. At the time we had no idea what these structures were, or that they had connections with paranormal phenomena. Since we began our research for this book, we have documented at least 100 of these structures in southern New York and Connecticut. Some of them have been used as storage sheds by local residents, but many of them are lost in the back country, slowly smothered by growing vegetation and destroyed by the roots of trees.

If you take a hike through the backroads of Putnam County, New York, there is a good chance that you will see one of these stone chambers. They are constructed of massive slabs of stone composed of granite, quartz, quartzite, limestone, and shale, which have been expertly cut and placed together with great precision. When the structure was completed, dirt was then placed on the top and the sides, giving the impression of a dark, gloomy doorway burrowing as much as forty feet into the earth. If you ask local residents who built them you will get a number of different answers: colonials, as root cellars; Native Americans as sweat lodges; and a controversial theory that they were built by ancient Middle Eastern and European explorers who came to the East Coast of the United States as long ago as 3,000 years. Our research into the origin of these structures began a great personal adventure, and also started a controversy in many scientific fields of study, especially archeology.

The Beginning of the Story

As stated earlier, we became interested in the chambers as a result of the UFO sightings in the area. Between 1983 and 1987 the sightings were so numerous in southern New York we were able to plot them on a map. The reports were classified into two different types, the first was a sighting of the object as it passed overhead or within close proximity of the witness. The majority of the cases investigated of this type were Close Encounters of the First Kind (CE-I), that is, seeing a UFO within 600 feet. Since the Hudson Valley UFO was so large most of the witnesses got a good look at it, even though it was at least 1,000 feet in altitude. We also labeled these cases also as CE-I.

To gain a better understanding of a report classified as CE-1, the following is an example given by Mr. Ed Burns, an IBM executive. This occurred on March 24, 1983, at approximately 8:30 P.M. He, along with an estimated 3,000 people, reported the same sighting that night while driving north on the Taconic State Parkway.

> I was driving home when I spotted a formation of lights off to my right. I became concerned because this looked like a very large aircraft that was in trouble and attempting an emergency landing. I continued to drive and the lights became more pronounced. They then came right over my car, I shut the radio off and rolled down the window and looked at this huge craft above me. I heard no noise. It was moving silently and slowly. When I reached the Millwood area, I noticed twelve cars off to the side of the road. I pulled over and stopped, and then all of a sudden this huge craft was right over my car. That's when it was really shocking. The craft then stopped. I looked up and saw that there were bright white lights with a number of different color lights in between them. The different colored lights then went off and all I saw was just the white lights. It was now hovering and I still heard no sound and this made it seem very eerie.
>
> So I just stood there watching it and the object just stood still in the sky like it was watching us. The guy next to me was just staring at it, so I started rambling on to him about how excited I was. He just looked at me and never said a word, it was like he was in shock or some kind of trance. The craft hovered there for about a minute or two then it started to move once again, going up the Taconic Parkway in a sort of a zigzag pattern. It still was moving very slowly and then all of a sudden it just shot forward and was now quite far from me. This object was triangular in shape and had at least forty lights on it. It was huge! All I could think about at this point was getting home to my family since I thought there was some kind of an invasion.

Infinity Sign in the Sky

The case above is a typical "common" UFO report, if such reports can be thought of as common, yet there are much more bizarre incidences on record. The second type of report is called "High Strangeness" and is much more than an encounter with an unidentified object. High Strangeness reports are paranormal events that center around UFO activity. These events include the appearance of humanoid creatures, electromagnetic effects, unusual sounds, poltergeist activity, strange light phenomena, the appearance of phantom-like entities, and lastly a variety of psychic phenomena. An example of a High Strangeness case is presented below. The report is interesting because there was not only the sighting of a UFO-like objects, but also electromagnetic effects and the materialization of a ghost-like entity. The case took place near Route 301 in the town of Kent Cliffs, New York, which is located in the heart of Putnam County. It must be noted that there are several of the stone chambers on the street where the witness lived at that time. The date of the incident was October 20, 1985 at 11:30 P.M. Below is a brief account as told to us in June of 1986 by a Mr. Robert Markell, a postal worker, and his family.

> It was about nine in the evening. My wife and daughter were watch-ing TV, when all of a sudden there was static interfering with the reception. We don't have cable and sometimes aircraft will cause lines through the picture, but I didn't hear a plane. Then all of a sud-den the lights went out in the house and I heard an unusual buzzing sound. The sound continued getting louder and louder. I thought at first a transformer down the street was on fire and ready to blow, so I became somewhat concerned. I put my shoes on and went outside, it seemed that the entire neighborhood was without power. I looked up into the sky and saw three balls of red light close to my house. Each of these lights were round and about the size of a golfball at arm's length. I continued to watch them for several seconds then they did a sort of dance in the sky. I then called for my wife and daughter to come out and see it.
>
> As they came outside, the lights all did a sort of infinity sign in the sky and merged together and became one ball of red light which then shot straight up in the sky. At that moment the lights came on in the

house and several of the light bulbs just exploded. That wasn't all, the TV came on full blast and later we found out that the washer down in the basement went on and went through the entire cycle with no clothes in it. This was a very strange thing to see happen, and my daughter was terrified. I tried to calm her down and explain that it was only a power surge, she didn't understand, since she is only ten years old. I was glad that the surge or whatever it was did not roast the wires in the house and start a fire.

I have this stone structure on my property [a chamber] and as I was going in the house I looked to the right because something caught my eye. I saw a glowing figure that looked like in was in a Revolutionary soldier outfit walk into the chamber. To me, it looked like a ghost, so I cautiously walked down my steps to the chamber and looked in. I felt very strange, my hair was standing up on my neck, but I saw nothing. I know what I saw, I heard a story that some of these things were used to house soldiers that passed through the area during colonial time. I also heard that many of the wounded and dead were placed in these things in the winter until the ground was soft enough so they could be buried. I think that I saw some type of ghost of a Revolutionary war soldier who perhaps died in battle.

Bizarre Findings

These two cases are typical of the many reports we have collected over the past seventeen years, giving us considerable data to work with. As previously stated, we decided to plot the reports on two maps. On the first we included 550 UFO cases of the Hudson Valley reported to us from 1983–1990, where the majority of cases were Close Encounters of the First Kind. On the second map we plotted 31 High Strangeness cases that seemed to be centered around some type of UFO activity. The first map revealed no pattern to the sightings, but the majority of the reports came from the Putnam County towns of Putnam Valley and Kent Cliffs, New York. The second map was a different story since it showed that the majority of High Strangeness cases were concentrated in clusters in Putnam, Dutchess, and Westchester counties of New York. (See Appendix 2: Tables and Charts, for a breakdown of the locations by town, page 134.)

The map of High Strangeness cases greatly intrigued us. Why were all of these paranormal occurrences concentrated in such small clusters less than a mile in diameter? Stranger still, the majority of the clusters were located in Kent Cliffs, New York. Our next step was to visit these locations to see what we could find. This was no easy task, since some were located in heavily wooded areas and in the isolated hills of Putnam County.

Over the next several years we spent considerable time trekking through miles of brush, looking for answers. Since the locations were almost impossible to cover with only two people, we put an exploratory team together. We had three teams of two or more people with a base camp usually set up at the road were the cars were parked. In spite of the thick overgrowth in many of the areas that we explored, and the threat of picking up a tick carrying Lyme disease, we ventured on. What we found made the trips well worthwhile. We uncovered a mystery that would make the Hudson Valley UFO case even stranger and, in time, answer some of our questions.

The Stone Chambers

In just about the center of every site of a cluster of High Strangeness reports we found an array of carved standing stones or several stone chambers. The structures were made by someone who had not only a great knowledge of stone cutting, but also of engineering, due to the way the weight of the capstones give stability to the walls. We also noticed that at some locations a number of the stones had strange markings on them. Further research has shown this to be of an ancient form of writing called Ogam. Ogam was first deciphered in Ireland during the seventeenth century, and it is a complete language written in a sort of Morse code. During our investigation we discovered that ten years before our find Dr. Barry Fell[1] claimed to have found similar inscriptions in a chamber in the same area. According to Dr. Fell, the inscriptions were translated as a prayer giving dedication to the Celtic God Bel, and the festival of fire called Beltaine. This was the first evidence that we had that these structures were very old and possibility

---

1 Dr. Fell's worked is documented in his book, *America B.C.*, Penguin Books, 1979.

of Celtic origin. But why were they built in New York and what was their connection to the UFO phenomenon?

We talked with a number of people about their origin. We also spend countless hours cataloging the chambers, and recording information about their physical features. Much of our time was spend at the local museums and historical societies looking for answers. There were mixed opinions, no one seemed to know for sure who constructed them. It seems they have been around for so long that they were indeed "lost in time."

CHAPTER 2

Before Columbus

HUMAN BEINGS, BY NATURE, love a mystery. However it has been said that the best part of a mystery is solving it. The stone chambers and their connection to paranormal phenomenon offered a mystery that was both intriguing and puzzling. As we tried to find answers for questions, ten more would arise. Who built them? How old are they? What was their purpose? Our research led us to many possibilities, and we had to explore all of them, from the simplest to the most bizarre.

Our Search Begins

We began our search at many of the local libraries and historical societies, but we could find no reference to the stone chambers in any of the material that was written during colonial times. What was even more puzzling was the fact that the chambers in the Hudson Valley of New York are not mentioned in any archeological book or any book that documented colonial life in New York. There was just no written record of their existence, except from the stories of local residents. During our search we did find a reference in *The History of Westchester County, New York,* a book that was published at the turn of the nineteenth century. The book documented some of the more interesting sights in the county and a special reference was made to the Balanced Rock in North Salem, New York (see color plate 3). The author of the book compared the rock with many similar megalithic structures found in Ireland, which have been verified of Druid origin. As a matter of record, the phrase "of Druid origin" was used in the text. (We will cover the Balanced Rock in greater detail later in chapter 9, since it would become the focus of our research.) This information gave us our first indication that the chambers, and many standing stones, were very old.

A Faded Letter

While doing research at the library at the Pound Ridge Historical Museum, we found a very faded letter dated July, 1742. A priest was writing a note to a local resident (name unknown) giving advice about a strange "stone hut" that the person, a farmer, found in the woods near his property. The priest advised him to stay away from it because it was the work of the devil. We found this statement strange.

If these things were nothing more than root cellars built in the eighteenth century, then why was the priest telling his parishioners to stay away from them? We began to realize that the chambers were there long before the colonial settlers arrived, and although they found many of them when they arrived, they stayed away from them.

The European Connection

The stone chambers we found in New England were in fact very similar to the chambers found in Ireland and Brittany, which are known to be of Celtic origin. The Celtic beliefs were regarded as the "old religion," and when Christianity flourished in Europe (due to the rise of the Holy Roman Empire) the old Celtic beliefs were not held in high regard by the church. Since the old ways were very widespread and deep-rooted, the church of Rome over a period of time slowly reeducated the people who were under Roman rule.

By the Middle Ages, the old Celtic religion was considered evil and the work of the devil. One of the reasons why the oldest Christian churches in Ireland and Brittany are built over ancient sacred Celtic ground is that the Christians had hoped to "counter the old gods" with the "power of the church." This could also be the reason why many holidays in Christendom follow the Celtic high holidays, the purpose being to smother the old Celtic gods and beliefs, which by the Middle Ages were considered to be associated with paganism, and outlawed by the Church.

Archaeologists Confronted

We decided to find out what local archaeologists thought about the chambers. We attended a meeting of the Archaeological Society at Norwalk Community College in Norwalk, Connecticut. During the meeting, researchers presented information on local Native American finds, and we heard a great number of "wows" when simple things like small pieces of flint and shell were presented to the group, with at least twenty or more slides documenting each find.

At break time, we talked to the president of the Society, who at the time was the Assistant State Archaeologist of Connecticut. We showed him a number of pictures of the stone chambers and he replied with a laugh, "Colonial root cellars." Then we showed him a picture of the Balanced Rock. He laughed and said, "Oh, you must be into the crazy theories of Barry Fell." (Dr. Fell's work is mentioned in chapter 1.) Phil then asked what he thought of the North Salem, New York, Balanced Rock. He replied, "Nothing more than an erratic left over from the Ice Age." (An *erratic* is a large rock that is pushed by a glacier and left in an area where boulders are not common. The rock is also not native to the area and sometimes it is perched on top of smaller rocks giving a very unusual appearance.)

Phil has a strong background in geology and he knew that the Balanced Rock was not a glacial erratic. The pedestal stones that hold the rock in place are carved and cone-shaped. The stone is perfectly placed atop the pedestal stones to distribute the weight evenly. Also, the base of the supporting stones form a triangle with the base exactly 5.44 feet. We found this truly amazing since a unit of measurement used during the Bronze Age was a yardstick that measured 2.72 feet. Today archaeologist call this the "megalithic yard." The megalithic yard was used to measure distance and it was also used in construction. All structures built during that time used the megalithic yard, or multiples of it. The length of the base of the Balanced Rock is exactly the standard megalithic yard times two! We found this too coincidental to be done by a glacier. How could a glacier prop that huge stone perfectly on top the pedestal stones using an ancient unit of measurement to achieve perfect weight distribution? The Society's president then walked away still chuckling under his voice, shaking his head. It seemed to us that he wanted to avoid any further conversation and did not want to even discuss the subject of the possible theories of the origin of the Balanced Rock or the stone chambers. It was as if we had just cornered a hard-nosed astronomer and asked him if he thought that UFOs were in fact alien spaceships. However, unlike UFOs, the chambers were there for all to see and although many of the archaeologists present knew of their existence, not one of them was willing to go on record to discuss them. When some of the younger graduate students talked about them with us, they whispered, fearing that their mentors would hear the discussion.

Was This the Scientific Method?

Not one person at the meeting would discuss the chambers with us in detail; it was apparent that the subject was taboo among New England archaeologists. The chambers were treated as if they did not exist since they did not fit in current theory. We found this attitude strange for a group of people with scientific backgrounds. Science is supposed to be the *pursuit* of truth, to search for answers to make known what is unknown.

It has been said that the most heinous offense a scientist can commit as a scientist is to declare something to be true that is not true. Nobel prize-winning scientist Robert Wilson, of Bell Labs, was referring to falsifying or inventing evidence, but he probably would agree that it is also a heinous offense for a scientist to declare that something does not exist when, in fact it may, especially if he or she has not attempted to determine its validity.

After a number of questions to several people we found out that no archaeologist present at this meeting studied or researched any of the chambers, yet they all had skeptical opinions. This is not the scientific method, and we were once again left without a professional opinion and continued to look for answers on our own. Later we were to connect with a number of professional and amateur researchers who, although they have been labeled as "radicals" by the scientific community, had definite ideas about the stone chambers and who built them.

Searching for Lost America

We were still confronted with the possibility, however slight and ridiculous it seemed, that the chambers were constructed in colonial times by farmers to store vegetables. Let's look at this a little more closely.

There are nearly 100 chambers alone in southern New York. They are in different states of decay, as if they were built over a long period of time. Some of the designs are different than others, since no two chambers are identical. If they were built within a span of twenty or more so years, then all the chambers would be weathered just about equally. This is not the case. Some of the chambers seem as if they have been standing around for centuries longer than others. If the chambers were in fact built by colonial farmers for storage, then the sheer number of chambers would be much too great to account for the population at the time.

When you examine any chamber, you will see that they were not easy to construct; their design is incredibly complex. The walls are usually constructed with a variety of different stones arranged in a *corbelled* manner (an architectural design used to support arches, parapets, and floors, in this case the walls which are made up of piles of stones arched inward to support the ceiling lintel stones). The walls in the chamber angle inward about 20 degrees of arc with the ceiling. The ceiling stones are huge flat slabs of rock that seem to have been chiseled out from nearby bedrock. From their design, it appears that the weight of the ceiling stones pressing down on top of the walls gives them a great deal of stability.

The majority of the stone chambers are constructed of granite with fine grain quartz, also shale, limestone, and quartzite have also been found to make up the doorways and walls. The majority of the chambers point to the south and are either east or west of the 180-degree compass mark. This would make sense if they were used by ancient explorers as shelter since the sun would shine inside the chamber most of the day and the back of the chamber would point to the north to help block out the cold northwest wind in winter.

According to Dr. Sal Trento, a professor at Lesley College in Massachusetts, the chambers in New York and the rest of New England are definitely not root cellars built by colonial farmers. Dr. Trento told us in an interview: "They are not colonial in nature, they were not used as root cellars. When you put vegetables in these things, they rot!" Dr. Trento admits that he has no idea who built them, but is sure that they are very old, and most of them predate Columbus. He told us that a shard of carbon found in one chamber in Massachusetts was radiocarbon dated to A.D. 500, almost 1,000 years before the Columbus voyage. He carefully pointed out that this date gives us an idea of when the chamber was used, but it does not tell us exactly when it was constructed. It is Dr. Trento's opinion that the chambers in southern New York are much older. He was dismayed that no one was studying them, since they are an archaeological enigma. Dr. Trento's early work on the New England stone chambers was published in his 1976 book *The Search for Lost America*.

Explorers from Atlantis?

We now had to focus our research into other possibilities. If the answer was not the obvious, then the answer must lie in an explanation that is not. We were then introduced to Carl Barton, a graduate of Yale university and a retired geologist. For twenty years he has been studying the stone chambers and standing stones in New England. He has a collection of what appears to be carved stones with scratches on them he claims is ancient Ogam. Barton believes that the chambers are situated over areas of high energy, and were used by a very ancient people as temples. He then began to show us hundreds of photographs he took of the chambers in southern New York. He pointed to a number of photographs that had a brilliant glowing white area, which he claimed are sections of the chambers giving off energy.

As we studied each photograph, our first impression was that they were nothing more than sunlight reflecting off sections of the rock causing an overexposure effect. However, as we looked closely at several more photographs, we could see that in some of them the sun was behind a hill or trees and there was no obvious explanation for the "energy-like" glowing effect that we saw on some of the prints. Eventually we got similar images during our photographic surveys; however, the cause at the time was completely unknown to us. Barton then began to tell us of his theory of who built the chambers and what they were used for.

Mysterious Physical Effects

Barton believed that many of the structures were the product of the Atlantians who fled to North America after the sinking of their continent. "The people from Atlantis," he told us, "did not build the chambers, but they marked the areas of high energy with standing stones (Figure 2.1). These standing stones harnessed the energy from the Earth and focused it. Later, when the area was explored by the Celts, they found these areas of high energy still marked by the standing stones and built temples (chambers) over them." Although this theory seemed very farfetched to us, we had to consider all possibilities. There is no doubt that the location in which the chambers reside generate some type of energy. Compass readings are deviated and there is a direct physical and mental effect on the people who visit them. On numerous occasions, people who have visited the chambers reported feeling drained of energy, or having a headache. At other locations visitors reported that they felt elated, euphoric, and full of energy. This energy in and around the chambers seem to have a greater effect on people who are empathic or who have other psychic abilities.

FIGURE 2.1 Standing stone, Route 116, Patterson, New York.

Several years ago we took a number of people to see a chamber located in the town of Southeast, New York. The chamber sits on one of the largest magnetic anomalies in all of Putnam County. (This magnetic anomaly has been confirmed by the last Geophysical Survey and the data is available from the scientific record archives in Washington, D.C.) As we explored the chamber, standing stones, and ancient walls in the area, several people who are well-known New York City psychics stated that they felt pressure on their heads. Out of the ten people who were with us that day, eight of them reported some type of sensation that ranged from feeling weak to a severe headache. At the end of the day we all went home feeling quite drained. The next day Phil called each member of the party and found out that everyone was in a state of depression and fatigue. Even Phil felt this and it took two days for him to feel fully recovered. Phil proposed a theory that the magnetic anomaly in the area may have been so great that it actually magnetized the iron in our blood cells, causing a sort of temporary anemia. Whatever the answer was, there was a very real effect on just about everyone present that day.

The Cathedral Chamber

Another chamber that seemed to always have a positive effect on those who stand in its center is one of the few in Kent Cliffs, New York. Because it is oval in shape and has a high ceiling, we named it the "Cathedral Chamber." This chamber has also had many reports of paranormal phenomena, including the appearance of ghost-like entities and unseen forces striking people who enter it.

On one occasion when we visited this chamber, Phil had a very bad headache. After staying in the chamber doing work cataloging the type of stone, he reported that his headache was gone and he felt full of energy and was anxious to continue taking measurements in more chambers. It is in this chamber that we found an inscribed stone that gave evidence that this structure may have been built by ancient Celts under the direction of a Druid priest. We will talk about this chamber in greater detail in chapter 3.

Beyond the Pillars of Hercules

Modern archeology would have us believe that North America remained isolated for hundreds of centuries, and that the first explorers from Europe were a number of brief visits by Vikings somewhere around A.D. 1200, but this is most likely not the truth. Ancient scrolls from Phoenicia that have been dated around 480 B.C. tell of Phoenician trading and exploration with the lands beyond the Pillars of Hercules. In 400 B.C., Plato tells of a land called Atlantis and other continents that lie "beyond the great ocean." The great Greek philosopher Theopompus, in 378 B.C., describes an island of immense size beyond the great ocean (the Atlantic) inhabited by strange people quite different from the Greeks. In 360 B.C., Aristotle also wrote about a land beyond the Pillars of Hercules, which was fertile and had many navigable rivers. The Phoenician writer Diodorus, in 21 B.C., describes a great country many days' journey across the Atlantic with vast forests and fruits. He says that it was discovered by the Phoenicians hundreds of years ago (hundreds of years before *his* time) and that they kept its existence a secret.

There is no doubt that many Celtic people and the ancient Greeks knew that North, and perhaps even South, America existed, and some of these cultures at that time had the seafaring technology to cross the Atlantic Ocean. Current evidence suggests that the exploration of North America from the "Old World" that took place before Columbus, and the Norsemen began the journey around 2000 B.C. and continued to around A.D. 800. Then for some unexplained reason there was a 400-year gap until about A.D. 1200 when Vikings, again, landed in North America. What was the reason why so many ancient cultures over such a long period of time were willing to brave the stormy Atlantic to come to North America?

There are two reasons why human beings explore: out of curiosity, and for money. During the Bronze Age there was a great call for bronze to make weapons and tools. If you want to make bronze, then you need copper and tin. By 1200 B.C. the copper was just about mined-out in Spain and the mountains of the Mediterranean. Many cultures, including the Celts of Europe, the people of the Iberian peninsula, and perhaps the ancient Greeks, sent out parties to explore new lands and look for riches and natural resources to help expand their own empires.

About 3,000 years ago bands of roving Celtic mariners may have crossed the North Atlantic to discover North America. They came from Spain and Portugal by way of the Canary Islands, sailing the trade winds and then filling their sails with the gales of the Gulf Stream to finally reach landfall in southern New England. They most likely sailed up the Hudson River, landing on the east side, and began their exploration of this strange new world. It is these people who, in fact, built many of the chambers in New York. Here they found a land that was rich in the iron ore, copper, and other minerals they needed. They also discovered vast forests with abundant wildlife, which they trapped to make leather and fur skins for clothing. Later, Celtic and early Christian explorers from Ireland took a different route across the North Atlantic to the Davis Strait, and finally to northern New England. It was these later explorers who came down the St. Lawrence River and upper Long Island Sound to build the chambers in Connecticut, Vermont, Massachusetts, and New Hampshire.

Everybody Built These Things

James Whittall, an amateur archaeologist and the director of the Early Sites Research Society, has been researching the stone chambers for over twenty-seven years. According to Whittall, material found inside chambers located in New Hampshire have been radiocarbon dated from A.D. 1100 to 1300. He told us: "We must be cautious about this data since this evidence suggests that these chambers were used during this time frame, but it does not give an indication as to when they were actually built." According to Whittall, not many artifacts were actually found, which tells us that these areas were a stopping place, and not used as living quarters for a great deal of time. Whittall said, "An overwhelming amount of data suggests there were Europeans here beginning at least as early as A.D. 500, although I don't think the pre-Colonials ever had an extended settlement."

According to the Early Sites excavation teams, there are about 400 stone chambers in New England and New York. A small percentage were clearly built by colonials, and some were used or remodeled by colonists or Native Americans. Most of the chambers have been found near inland waterways or former Indian trails. There has been indication that some of the chambers may have been used by the Indians as sweat houses. When we asked him who built them he replied, "Everybody built these things." During our research at the New York City Public Library we came across a very old tale of an adventurous Irish monk who crossed the Atlantic to North America almost a thousand years before Columbus.[1] He was known as Saint Brendan the Navigator, and his story may have actually inspired Columbus to undertake a journey that would have been considered impossible for the time. The tale of St. Brendan follows, our comments analyzing the adventure appear in italics.

---

1 *Navigatio Sancti Brendan. The Voyage of St. Brendan,* A story from the early 12th century, Oxford Press, 1928.

Brendan the Navigator, and his Voyage

St. Brendan was born approximately in the year A.D. 489 in County Kerry, Ireland. Even as a child, Brendan had a very inquisitive mind and quickly mastered the arts and sciences. While still a child, several miracles were attributed to him, such as making spring water appear during a drought, locating precious metals under the ground, and ridding his village of fleas. Because of his abilities, Bishop Erc, the monk in charge of a local monastery, took Brendan to raise in the priesthood. While still a young man, Brendan became head of a community of 3,000 monks in a monastery at Clonfert. One day an older monk named Barrind told Brendan that he had sailed across the ocean and visited an incredible land that was a paradise. Intrigued by this story, Brendan decided to build a ship and sail toward the setting sun in search of this land that was only known as Paradise.

Saint Brendan went to the top of the mountain behind the monastery, fasted, and meditated for forty days, seeking guidance on what to do. At the end of the forty days, he came down off the mountain and asked fourteen monks to accompany him on the journey; they all promptly volunteered. For weeks they labored to build the boat. It was a wood-framed boat, covered in oak-bark tanned ox-hides, and they smeared the joints with fats from animals to seal them. The boat had large square sails, and when they were ready to set sail, they filled it with as many provisions as they could carry and extra hides. On the day that they were ready to sail, three more monks approached them and pleaded to Brendan to let them join their expedition. Brendan looked at each of them and had a vision that two of them would die on the voyage, and one would not return of his own free will. In spite of the dire prophecy, the three monks still joined the band of adventurers. Several days before the boat was completed, Brendan was shown in a dream that to reach the land called Paradise he would have to sail toward the west. However, instead of going west, the ocean currents took them north (see map, Figure 2.2, next page).

They sailed for fifteen days and came upon a tall rocky island with waterfalls cascading down the sides of the cliffs. They navigated into a

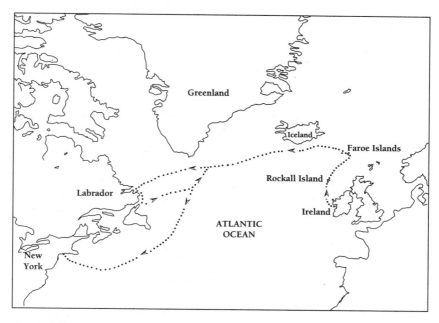

FIGURE 2.2 St. Brendan's Voyage across the Atlantic to North America.

small inlet and the crew disembarked from the ship onto a beach in the hopes of finding food. Then something strange took place. They were greeted by a small dog who lead them to an area where food was laid out for them, just as if someone were expecting them. For several days they would wake up to find fresh food and drink, and although they never saw anyone place the food, it was waiting for them each morning. One morning Brendan woke up early hoping to get a glimpse of their secret benefactor. As he watched in the darkness he saw a figure that he recognized as one of the monks he had seen in his vision at the beginning of the voyage. The monk seemed to be talking to someone as if bargaining or arranging some type of deal. Brendan then saw a shadowy dark figure enter the monk's body. The next day Brendan confronted the man and told him he was aware of the deal he had made with the devil for food in exchange for his soul. Brendan confronted the demon and as the demon left the monk's body, Brendan struck down the monk, killing him. Then as they were getting ready to leave the island, a handsome young man appeared out of nowhere and provided them with bread and water. He told Brendan that the voyage ahead was filled with hardship and danger.

> *Let us take a moment to analyze what we just covered. It seems that from a very early age Brendan was gifted with psychic abilities. He also was without doubt a prodigy in the arts and sciences. He always felt different from everyone else and entered into the priesthood at an early age. In the fifth century to become a priest at such an early age was very difficult, Brendan must have been quite gifted. As he began his journey, Brendan apparently attempted to head west, because he was sure that this land he knew of as Paradise existed across the vast ocean. According to our calculations and research using maps showing oceanographic currents, Brendan's ship, after heading west for 150 miles, was turned north by the North Atlantic drift. After sailing in the current for about twelve more days he reached a small island. According to our research, and assuming that the ship traveled forty miles a day and that he continued in the current mentioned above, the first stop for Brendan would have been would have been the island of Rockall, which is 250 miles northwest of Scotland.*
>
> *If one were to read the Brendan story they might come to the conclusion that most of it is unbelievable and is just a myth, especially the part were they encountered the demon and the miraculous appearance of the food. We have to remember that much of the translation of the Brendan story is taken from the ancient Irish language and the exact translation, word-for-word, makes the story sound more like a fairy tale than reality. However, it is very possible that other forces were involved in helping Brendan. The strange shadowy figure, the young boy, and even the dog could have been some type of beings sent by a higher intelligence to help Brendan complete his voyage. After spending several days on the island, they then left Rockall and once again set their sail westward.*

The Journey Continues

They continued their voyage, and the warning that the young man gave them came to pass. For three months they braved the elements and fought against the wind. The entire crew was nearly in a state of exhaustion when they finally spotted land. They were greeted by a quiet white-haired elder very close to where their ship achieved landfall. They were joined by eleven monks who offered them food and washed their feet. Although there were gestures of friendship, the monks remained silent.

The head monk or abbot finally broke the silence to tell Brendan that the loaves of bread that he was eating were miraculously brought to them and the candles in the chapel never burned away. Brendan was told that all twenty-four monks in the monastery never ate any cooked food. He also said that they had been on the island for over eighty years, and that they followed a vow of silence. Brendan seemed very surprised because not one of the monks seemed old. He was told by the abbot that they never aged, or were bothered by evil spirits. Brendan was also told that they arrived at the island a very long time ago to escape the evils of the world, to isolate themselves and become pure in the image of God. Brendan and his shipmates stayed at the island until after Christmas, and then left, ready to continue their journey to find Paradise.

After leaving Rockall island, it seems strange that they should have spent such a long time at sea. The only explanation is that they were caught in the gyre currents of the North Atlantic drift then pushed back by the opposing currents further north from Iceland. The denser cold water from this area creates a very powerful stream of water that would have pushed Brendan's ship backward once again to the North Atlantic drift where he could have gone in circles for months. Finally, due to winds from the west, his ship then could have been pushed northwest to the Faroe Islands, which are about 200 miles from northern Scotland. The islands are actually a group of twenty-four islands, and today seventeen are inhabited. It is thought that they were settled by Irish monks between A.D. 500 and 700. It seems that Brendan may have landed first on the most southerly one. This would be the logical place for the monks to build a monastery since it is still within reach of the British Islands, but far enough away so that they can remain isolated from the rest of humanity.

The monks on this island were strange indeed. The first thing they did when they greeted them was to wash the feet of Brendan and his comrades. This is a very old practice that originated during the time of Christ. There are legends of groups of people who isolated themselves from the rest of the world to mediate and achieve spiritual enlightenment. According to legend these "monks" stayed on a particular diet and found some secret elixir of life so that they never aged or became ill. In Brendan's time it was thought that all illness were in fact caused by evil spirits. This is what the abbot could have meant when he told Brendan that they were "not bothered by evil spirits." It is possible that the monks on the island were looked out for by a group of supernatural or alien beings from a higher technology. This would account for their miraculous food supply and the "candles" that never burned out. Perhaps the "candles" were, in fact, some type of electric lights.

The Islands of Sheep and Birds

After leaving the monks, a very short time later they landed on an island with many large streams full of big fish, called the Island of Sheep, because large sheep ran wild all year around. They stayed on the Island of Sheep until Easter and then traveled to a nearby island. This island was stony without grass, and as they began to built a fire, the island began to shake and move. The monks scrambled back onto the boat in a frenzy as they watched the "island" move away with their fire still burning on it. Saint Brendan told them that it was a giant fish called Jasconius. The monks then traveled to another nearby island called The Paradise of Birds, where they followed a narrow channel to the center of the island. They saw a vast tree covered with a multitude of white birds. The birds sang as if they were chanting verses. Brendan told the monks the birds were actually the spirits of men who had fallen from the grace of God and are now trying to be forgiven by singing the praises of the Lord. Brendan then heard a voice that sounded like it came from the birds saying that it would be seven years before he would reach the land he was looking for.

It seems Brendan and his monks traveled only a small distance on the next leg of their journey, that would keep them still in the Faroe Islands. Of the twenty-four islands that make up the chain, one is very well known for its large white sheep and another has many fabulous birds. The giant fish, Jasconius, most probably can be identified as a whale or perhaps some sort of ship they encountered at sea.

We are quite sure that Brendan may have had the help of unknown beings. Were they supernatural or extraterrestrial? The voice Brendan heard could have been once again a precognitive vision. From our own research, we have found that some psychics find it easier to tap into their abilities while listening to music that enhances the spirit. Saint Brendan often heard voices and, like Joan of Arc and many prophets of old, he claimed that the voices came from God. Today many people also hear voices that tell them of future events, but many of these people claim the voices do not come from God, but they come from extraterrestrials.

Close Encounter with a Sea Monster

According to the story, they then sailed for forty days and, on the fortieth day, they saw a huge sea monster following them. The monks panicked as the creature came closer and closer, for they thought they were going to be eaten alive. The monks cried out to Brendan to do something, because surely they felt that the creature was sent by the Evil One to end their voyage. Brendan began praying. Then out of nowhere, from the opposite direction, another beast appeared. The second beast cut off the path of the first beast before it reached the ship. Breathing fire, it cut the beast into three parts. After saving Brendan and his men, the beast swam away and was soon lost in the distance. The monks then came upon a large wooded island and when they went ashore they found part of the dead sea monster. At this point Brendan and his crew were starving, and Brendan told them it was safe to eat the monster. The monks then were trapped on the island due to storms, rain, wind, and hail for three months before they were able to continue their journey.

It is very difficult to actually know what took place in the encounter with the "sea monster." If we look at the passage above from a logical point of view perhaps the sea monster that was ready to attack their boat was a great white shark. Great white sharks have been documented attacking boats and one that was made of animal skins and sealed with animal grease would certainly attract their attention. The second creature acted like it could have been a killer whale, who are also known for attacking sharks. The fire coming from the second beast that the men in Brendan's boat saw could easily be explained by the breath coming out of the blowhole of a killer whale, which looks like steam.

From our research, the wooded island that was Brendan's next stop was Iceland, which is known for its forests. The story says it took Brendan forty days to get there; normally under good circumstances it should have taken him less than fourteen days. Forty days is a time period often used in Biblical stories as a time frame set by God to cleanse the prophets. We have to assume that perhaps the trip took them less than forty days. There is no doubt that it took Brendan a great deal longer than it should have to reach Iceland since his crew ran out of food and water. It seems that he was caught in the ocean currents for an unknown length of time. The monks were stuck on the island for three months because of wind and hail, so we *can assume that he reached Iceland sometime in the winter and stayed there till spring.*

The Strange Island

As the weather improved, Brendan and his crew were able to leave the island (Iceland) and once again head out to sea. After a length of time they came upon a uncommonly flat island that was barely above sea level. The island had no trees or other forms of vegetation, but the surface was covered with purple and white fruit. As they were gathering the fruit, a group of young boys dressed in white, older boys dressed in blue, and elders dressed in purple, approached them. They gave Brendan a large basket of purple and white fruits, and in exchange for the food they asked one of the latecoming monks to stay with them. Brendan gave his permission for the monk to stay and the rest of the crew raised the ships sails and once again headed out to sea. They were able to squeeze a pound of juice from each fruit which was enough food to feed each man for twelve days.

> *After Brendan and his crew left Iceland, the ocean currents would have taken his ship to the southwest toward North America. There are no islands in the Atlantic ocean in this direction between Iceland and Newfoundland. The flat island could have been something artificial, perhaps some type of large ship since it also had people on it. We must assume that perhaps Brendan's voyage was assisted by a higher intelligence, extraterrestrials, angels, or whatever you want to call them. Here on the "island" they were given food and met with a group of people in different colored clothes. These people asked in exchange for the food that one of the monks stay with them. The monk who they wanted to stay was one of the three that Brendan saw in his vision not returning with them. Perhaps it was the monk's destiny to meet these beings on this "island" and go with them, or was it the earliest recorded UFO abduction? Whoever the beings were in the large ship on the ocean, they gave Brendan and his men enough supplies to continue their journey. Whatever the mysterious fruit was it provided enough food to feed each of his crew for twelve days. It must have been a very high source of protein, and we know of no purple and white fruit that can provide enough food for a human being for this long of a period. Therefore we must assume that the fruit could have been not of this*

world. There are many legends of the food of the gods that when eaten by mortals would give them extraordinary powers and provide sustenance for a long period of time.

The Kind "Bird"

Several days into their voyage, Brendan realized that the next landfall was very far off and they may not have enough food to continue their journey. A number of days then passed and as the food supplies diminished something appeared in the sky that looked like a bird. The bird dropped a branch into the boat which was covered with bright red grapes the size of apples. They lived off the fruit for eight days and then three days later they came across an island that was covered with the same fruit. They stayed there for forty days.

We can only speculate what the bird actually was. In biblical times anything referred to as a bird or cloud indicated some type of aerial object. Perhaps the bird was actually some type of remote-controlled probe which was sent by the beings that they last encountered on the "flat island" to bring them more food, check on their progress, and to show them the direction that they should go. We think that Brendan and his crew then landed somewhere on the east coast of Labrador, either on the main coastline or one of the many islands offshore. Once again they stayed for forty days, but we really can't accept this number as fact.

The Iceberg

After returning to sea with their boat filled with many different kinds of fruits, they came across a stretch of water so clear that they could see the bottom. It took eight days to cross the patch of clear sea. Sometime later they observed a shiny pillar in the distance, so they turned their ship to sail toward it, but it took them three days to reach the pillar. As they approached the pillar, they saw a passageway through it. They took down their sails so they could fit. As they passed through, they noticed that the pillar extended deep into the water as far as they could see. The pillar was actually a floating island that was like bright crystal, but harder than marble, and the water was clear as glass. They left the pillar, set their sails, and headed north for eight days.

*The pillar was so intriguing that it caused Brendan and his crew to leave
land and once again head out to sea. They approached the "pillar" to see
that it extended deep into the water. As water gets colder it becomes
clearer, and you can see deeper into the depths. It seems that there could be
no doubt that this passage clearly refers to the sighting of an iceberg in the
North Atlantic. After leaving the iceberg they headed north which would
take them away from North America to Greenland.*

Fire and Brimstone

On the eighth day they came to a rocky, harsh island. However, as they
tried to steer away, the current pushed them toward it. As they neared the
island hot slag was thrown at them, which landed a few hundred feet
from the boat, sending up plumes of steam and causing the sea to boil.
They rowed as hard as possible to get away as more hot slag was hurled
at them. The entire island looked as if it was on fire and there was a hor-
rible stench. Brendan thought they had reached the edge of Hell.

They sailed away toward a mountain that was smoking and the ship
ran aground before the ship reached the land. The third latecoming
monk jumped from the boat in panic saying that he was powerless to
stop. As he ran to the base of a cliff screaming in terror, fiery demons
appeared and set him ablaze. The rest of the monks jumped back into
the boat and the wind carried them back out to sea. They then headed
south. As they looked back at the once-smoking mountain, it now
looked like a huge fire. Brendan had a vision and was told they would
have a forty-day journey before they would reach Paradise, and then
God would bring them safely back to Ireland.

*The area that Brendan was sailing through is noted for its volcanic activity.
We see evidence in the passage above we are dealing with submerged volcanoes and island volcanoes. The stench was probably sulfur dioxide, which is
a common volcanic gas and smells like rotten eggs. In medieval times the
smell of burning sulfur was always associated with the appearance of the
devil. We have no idea why the monk jumped from the boat into what seems*

to be a flow of hot ash and lava. Perhaps he was terrified and felt he had to get off the boat and run for his life. It is interesting to note that this was also one of the three monks who Brendan saw at the beginning of the voyage in a vision as not returning.

Paradise!

After forty days they found themselves in a great fog with very calm seas, when they finally found their way through the fog they came across land. Brendan recognized the smell of the place as the same as told to him by the monk Barrind. At last, Brendan had found Paradise. They spent forty days exploring, but never determined how large the land was. Then a messenger of God appeared to Brendan and told him he needed to return to Ireland to tell his story before he died. Brendan then gave instructions for his crew to gather provisions for the journey home.

When they returned to Ireland, Saint Brendan told all the monks what had happened during their journey and made detailed maps of the way to the new land beyond the great ocean. Brendan died shortly after that. Legend says that he lived to be ninety-three years old, and died peacefully in the monastery among his fellow monks.

Brendan landed somewhere on the coast of North America. The area just north of Long Island is noted for its intense fog banks. The ocean currents would have taken Brendan's ship down along the coast of North America and, looking for a safe haven, he could have navigated his boat through Long Island Sound, which is a very calm stretch of water when compared to the ocean. In conclusion of the story, the final question is: Was it possible for the people of Ireland to cross the Atlantic in the fifth century?

In the New York City Public library, where we did most of our research, we also came across a book called The Brendan Voyage, *written by a brave young man who was obsessed with the Brendan legend. He set out to prove that ships at that time were capable of an extended ocean voyage and the people who lived at the time of St. Brendan had the seafaring knowledge to make the journey.*

A Modern-Day Voyage

In the early 1970s, explorer Tim Severin was intrigued by the Brendan story and the possibility of crossing the Atlantic in a leather boat like the one used by Brendan in the fifth century. He spent years tracking down all the information on how to make such a boat and sail it. Many of the Irish people came to help him build a duplicate of the Brendan ship.

To construct the frame, he started with white wood of native Irish ash and then used heartwood of oak to finish. It took nearly two miles of leather thong to hand-lash the framework together. According to legend, the monks used oak-bark tanned leather for the skin of the boat, so Severin tried this and found it did actually outperform all the other leathers for this purpose. The grease from wool, a very plentiful resource both then and now, was used to seal the joints and waterproof the leather.

In 1976, Severin and his crew of three left Ireland in the boat, which was christened *The Brendan* in honor of the monk. They traveled approximately forty miles a day and reached Iceland before winter set in. However since the winter was severe that year they had to hold off until the next year to continue the voyage. In the spring of 1977 they returned to Iceland to finish what they had started. It took a total of three-and-a-half months to reach Newfoundland. Severin and his crew certainly proved that the Atlantic could be crossed in a ship in which Irish monks had at their disposal in the fifth century.

But where did Brendan land? One would think that if he spent forty days along the coast of New England he would have left something behind. After several months of research we found the remains of a settlement located in Groton, Connecticut, called Gungywamp, which may have been Saint Brendan's landing site.

CHAPTER 3

Remnants of a Lost People

*I*N ST. BRENDAN'S STORY, we see that a group of monks appear to have landed on the eastern shores of North America. From the research that we have done, we have come to the conclusion that Brendan and his monks steered their way into the northern end of Long Island Sound and came ashore near the area of North Groton, Connecticut. Within easy walking distance of the water is an area called Gungywamp, where a number ancient stone structures of unknown origin have been found. The complex covers an area of fifty-five acres and the topography of the land includes many ledges, rock outcropping, swamps, bogs, cliffs, and hills. It is densely wooded with second-growth trees and undergrowth.

We were met there by David Barron, president of the Gungywamp Society. He told us that since 1979, a combined group of people from the Gungywamp Society and NEARA (New England Antiquities Research Association) have been conducting surveys and excavations within the complex and the neighboring land. In May, 1994 they found sufficient information to make a formal presentation to the Smithsonian Institution in Washington, D.C. Apparently their presentation was convincing enough to have several gentlemen approach the group with the conclusion "we will have to go back to our offices and re-think American history."

During the excavation, they found many Native American artifacts along with the remains of two foundations on the property that were once colonial homes. The rest of the complex cannot be as easily explained and, according to current research, the structures predate colonial times. Dr. Barry Fell, whom we have mentioned earlier, visited the site and was able to identify several crude "Christograms" carved into rock. He predicted that, "Whenever you find a Christogram like this you are bound to find a number Chi Rhos." (Chi Rho: A symbol for Christ formed by superimposing the Greek letter P [Rho] over the Greek letter X [Chi] to form a combination symbol P and X. These letters come from the Byzantine–Greek word "Christos.")

Just three years after Fell's prediction, several anciently devised Chi Rho symbols were found. Several years later, David Barron took a trip with James Whittall to the British Isles in search of early Christian sites. During the course of their research they discovered several excellent references and drawings of early Chi Rhos. Using this information they were able to identify those in the North Gungywamp area as "Transitional Chi Rhos," having been in use between A.D. 500 and 700. This would place the Gungywamp symbols within the time frame of the Brendan voyage. Barron feels that this means that the Christian explorers were in the area long enough to expose the locals to the early Christian symbols.

We then began our journey to explore the wonders of Gungywamp. We started by following a well-defined path through the woods, where we encountered a series of unusual megalithic features, including a number of walls and standing stones. In this line of standing stones we saw the most amazing ideographic image of a bird of prey preparing to take flight. In the same area are numerous meandering walls that defy explanation. An interesting letter by John Pynchon on November 30, 1654, talks about these strange stone walls.[1] He is writing his mentor, John Winthrop, the younger. The following is a portion of that letter.

---

1 Letter obtained from Gungywamp study.

30 November 1654
Springfield

Honored Sir;

Understanding you are now at Newhaven, & supposing there will be
opportunity from Hartford for Conveyance thither, I make bold to scribble
a few lines to you . . .

Sir I heare a report of a stonewall and strong fort in it, made all of
Stone, which is newly discovered at or neere Pequet, (presently known as
the Gungywamp Range), I should be glad to know the truth of it from your
selfe, here being many strange reports about it.

John Pynchon

This letter gives us insight as what the people thought of the stone
structures at that time. Since the letter was dated 1654, we know these
walls and standing stones were not built in colonial times. Barron told
us that he has flown over the area to get an aerial view of the walls. He
found that the walls follow no pattern that a colonial farmer would use
to mark crops, paths, or property boundary areas.

The Hidden Chamber

Having gone past the stone walls and standing stones, we then entered
the main complex. There we saw no fewer than four semi-subter-
ranean dry stone-walled chambers (or ruins thereof). It is unfortunate
that no significant artifacts have been found to help date their construction. However, we heard a very interesting story about a small
chamber that was discovered by accident.

About twenty years ago a man and his brother were hiking through
the area, when they noticed something very odd. They saw a small
bird slip into a hole in the side of a small mound. Upon further investigation, they found a hidden entrance to a small stone chamber. Once
they opened it they discovered a small black pot on the dirt floor with
a bird's nest in it. The men took the pot out of the chamber, and, after
they cleaned out the bird's nest, brought it to the anthropology department at a local college. Several weeks later they returned to the chamber to see what the scientists found out. They were told that no one
had seen the pot for days and it was never found again. Both men felt

that the pot was made of bronze, but without the actual artifact they could prove nothing. Perhaps the content of the pot contained the remains of an Irish monk!

The Equinoctial Chamber

Almost within a stone's throw of this "hidden chamber" is the largest chamber that is fully intact. A hole built into the rear upper wall, called the "Illuminaire Shaft," was discovered by accident. It permits the equinoctial sunset to penetrate into the dark confines on two days of the year. The rays illuminate an entrance to a hidden beehive chamber located in the north wall of the chamber. The hidden extension was discovered by a couple who noticed an odd placement of rocks in that wall. This small beehive chamber that is attached to the larger is almost a third of the size of the main chamber.

Barron, who regularly gives tours of the complex at Gungywamp, is trying to teach people about our hidden past and preserve it for research at the same time. During some of these tours he reported that many people experience strange effects when entering the chamber. Some people feel dizzy, others lightheaded, some nauseated, and others may get a headache. During our trip there, Marianne felt nauseated almost immediately upon entering the chamber, and Phil had a mild headache. He brought in a group of visiting nurses, and they were so intrigued by this response that they spent a few Saturdays with Barron doing an experiment. They took everybody's blood pressure and heart rate in the parking lot, then again at this chamber, and finally a third time at a location called the "Cliff of Tears." They were amazed to find out that almost without exception, every everybody's vital signs were normal in the parking lot and had a significant decrease at the chamber and then an even higher decrease at the Cliff of Tears. At the end of the experiment the numbers returned to normal in the parking lot.

The Mill

We then walked a short way up a small, steep hill to see the so-called Tan Bark Mill. Pieces of charcoal found at this location were radiocarbon dated to about A.D. 500. This time frame has two significant meanings: first, it is the time that Brendan would have made his journey; second, it is the same time frame that the transitional Christograms and Chi Rhos were used by early Christian monks. The "Mill" is composed of two concentric circles of "worked" stone slabs (laid end to end), one circle resting within the bounds of the other; the inner circle with a diameter 8.85 feet, is composed of nine stones. The outer circle of stones has thirteen slabs and measures 10.82 feet in diameter. (It is interesting to note that the megalithic yard which we have mentioned before is 2.72 feet, and four times that is 10.88 inches.) All the stones have been worked to create a continuous curve, either convex or concave, in the face bordering the runnel. Although the outer circle has fallen away from its original position, a reconstruction by photographic analysis clearly shows that the runnel, separating the circles, was about 9 inches wide.

A noted NASA astronomer,[2] using alignments from the center of the circle of stones to a nearby recumbent (fallen stone marker), strongly suggests that the westerly horizon and the circle of stones line up neatly to provide for a "Venus Calendar." He suggested that more research and confirmation of various declinations would be needed to qualify the site for this unique distinction.

It is well known that such constructions were used for tanning, apple cider production, and lime shell crushing up to about A.D. 700. The Gungywamp Society offers the theory that it was most likely a tan bark mill used in the process of tanning leather. At the mill, tree bark was crushed, and then the pulverized product was placed into a pit containing water. The natural elements in the bark combined with the water to form tannic acid. At this point, animal skins were soaked in the solution for a period of days. The skins, which were now leather, were then taken out to a nearby location that had plenty of running water, and there they were rinsed. The final product was leather that was used for clothing, shoes, and other goods.

---

2 Information obtained from Gungywamp Society publications. Astronomer's name and position is on file.

The Cliff of Tears

The Cliff of Tears site is located just west of Slag Iron Creek on private property. It contains nineteen low, unpretentious stone cairns. It was incredible to see so many cairns located in such a small area. The cairns were built in odd shapes and sizes: circles, teardrops, ovals, squares, and rectangles. Each cairn appears to have its own "identity" in terms of the kind of rock or material used. It is obvious from seeing the cairns that these were not simple colonial field-clearing piles.

The most unique of these cairns is the boat-shaped cairn: it has three standing stones set at the bow, midship, and aft. Moving further along the path, the actual Cliff of Tears is located north of the cairn field. It is a stone outcropping rising dramatically into the air two hundred yards. The site itself was named because of its peculiar physiological effects on some visitors. One of these effects was the sudden onset of uncontrollable tears for no discernible reason. Other people have had spontaneous nosebleeds and others have even begun bleeding through their eyes, ears, and fingernails.

The Cliff of Tears has been the scene of many strange phenomena. Perhaps, the strangest story we ever heard took place there about ten years ago. The story was told to us by a local scientist in Connecticut who, with a party of five people, visited the Cliff of Tears one summer afternoon. Two members of this party experienced something that they would never forget. They were caught in some sort of "time dilation" that the other members of the party could not explain. This story is so strange that we will have to save it for chapter 8: "Doorways to Another Dimension."

Ancient Evidence

We now had some evidence that the Gungywamp complex could have been constructed around A.D. 500 by St. Brendan or his followers. We were still faced with a mystery. If the chambers in the Hudson Valley were much older than the Gungywamp complex and built over a longer period of time, who constructed them and what were they used for? We had to look for enough evidence to at least put together a theory.

We then called Dr. Robert Funk who, during the early 1990s was the New York State archaeologist. Dr. Funk informed us in a telephone conversation that the chambers are actually a sore thumb with archaeologist since "they don't fit in with current theory of early America." He told us: "They are sterile from an archeological point of view. Dr. Ken Feder of Central Connecticut State University dug in two chambers in the Hudson Valley in the late 1980s and found colonial artifacts, so we assume that they were constructed by colonial farmers as root cellars." Phil asked what sort of artifacts he found. "Well," Funk replied, "he found nails and metal clasps." Phil then asked how he knew they were colonial. The reply was that they were compared with nails used in the eighteenth century and were found to be almost identical.

This really puzzled us since we also have found pieces of metal in the chambers before and they were so covered with a crusty rust that it was impossible to tell the shape of the thing. Also, eighteenth century nails used in the United States and England were made the same as the nails used by the Celts in the British Isles during the fourth century A.D. We were informed that Dr. Fedar did not even bother to analyze the metal to determine its origin. This would have settled the dispute once and for all. Metals have a distinct molecular signature from the location from which they were mined. For example, iron in the northeast United States has a different spectroscopic molecular signature from iron mined in Spain. Even if some colonial artifacts were found in the chambers, that does not prove they were constructed by colonial farmers; it only proves that they used them for a period of time. We thought that this assumption was very unscientific for a person who has an excellent reputation as a field researcher.

The chambers are of magnificent construction, and according to several popular books on archeology, architecture is an artifact in itself since its design can be compared with different cultures at any given time period. Once again the only other place in the world that you find similar structures is in Ireland and Brittany, which are known to be of Celtic origin. Yet even faced with this evidence most local scientists still discount it as proof. Today garbage from the twentieth century is being thrown into the chambers and buried. Does this mean that in perhaps 300 years from now investigators will assume that they were built by twentieth-century suburbanites to store unwanted junk?

Dr. Funk then changed gears and stated that the chambers are not protected since they have not been labeled as historic or archaeological sites. We thought this was a very unusual comment since even if they are colonial we have no idea on how and why they were built. In Putnam County, New York, local and state archaeologists will go out of their way to fight to save and preserve a colonial barn. However, no one was willing to lift a finger to save the chambers, which are slowly being destroyed by vandalism, the elements, and the construction of homes in the area by high-powered land investors. Dr. Funk then told us that if one chamber was declared an archeological site, then you would have to declare them all. You see, many of the chambers are on land that is due to be developed and in order to "develop" the land you will have to level the grounds. This means that if there is a chamber on that property it will be destroyed.

We know for a fact that at least seventeen chambers have already been destroyed since 1982. A builder's nightmare is that during construction someone discovers an archaeological find on the land. This means that construction has to stop until a team of researchers can come in and determine what the find represents. Sometimes the investigation can take months. Although the construction has to stop, the developer still has to pay the crew and this could add up to hundreds of thousands of dollars. So you can see why we weren't exactly welcomed in some locations. At least one chamber was saved from the bulldozer thanks to the efforts of our research team and the Putnam County Historical Society. This chamber lies just off the road on Route 301 in Kent Cliffs, New York, and it was in this chamber that we found evidence that the Druids may have had a strong influence on the construction of some Hudson Valley stone chambers.

The Seven Sisters

As we stated earlier, the chambers seem to come in three basic shapes. The first type, and the most common, is a rectangle with a length

FIGURE 3.1 The Route 301 chamber.

between four and six times greater than the width. We call these chambers "galleries" since this is what they most resemble. The second and third type is oval and square, and we have found these chambers to be the rarest. We were told by an authority on Celtic beliefs that the two basic shapes, cylindrical and oval are the representation of male and female elements in nature.

There is some indication that the gallery chambers may have been used for shelter, storage, a calendar to show the equinoxes and solstices, and perhaps a sanctuary to hold a body before funeral rites. In some of the gallery chambers we found a slab of rock carved out of the bedrock near the rear of the chamber. The slab has been placed horizontally, and is large enough to hold the body of a full-grown man.

The chamber off Route 301 is of the oval type, with a high ceiling (see Figure 3.1, above). It is made up of large rocks of various types. In our investigation we found that some of the rocks were actually cut and fitted in place with expert precision. We also found numerous drill marks in some of the igneous rocks in the chamber. In many of the chambers, mortar can be seen between the rocks, which was placed there long after the structure was built. In several chambers we have found colonial mortar, which has a rich limestone base, and in others, modern-day cement.

It is interesting to note that the mortar or cement can be found falling off the rock and weathering greatly from the elements, but the chambers are still standing. The chamber off Route 301 had no mortar or cement on the walls indicating that it was not used by modern-day or colonial residents. This chamber was once hidden in the woods, and then about ten years ago the road was widened and now it is located on the shoulder of a major route in Putnam County. It was in this chamber that we found a cylindrical piece of limestone that was about a half meter high. The stone was carved in a conical shape and then smoothed perhaps using a fine grain dirt or sand. The stone was placed in the front upper left wall of the chamber on a shelf of flat slate that was doubtlessly made to hold it. At the bottom there were rows of some type of writing on the bottom. But what was most amazing was a number of markings in a very distinct pattern on the upper part of the stone.

When Phil examined the stone he quickly recognized the pattern as the small star cluster—the Pleiades—which is also known as "the Seven Sisters." The Pleiades can be easily recognized in the winter night sky, since it looks like a tiny Little Dipper. The seven stars that make up the small constellation shine with a beautiful luster giving them the appearance of blue-white gems in the sky. Some astronomy history buffs believe that the childhood rhyme, "Twinkle, twinkle, little star, how I wonder what you are, up above the world so high, like a diamond in the sky," was inspired by several bright stars and the Pleiades star cluster.

Also, on the stone was what looked like the representation of Aldebaran, the brightest star in Taurus the Bull, which is very close to the Seven Sisters. During our lectures we show a slide of the Seven Sisters taken by Phil and then compare it with the markings on the stone. There is no doubt about it—even the most skeptical can clearly see that someone was trying to represent the constellation and some of the stars of Taurus on the rock . . . *but who?*

The Druid High Holiday

When one looks at the Pleiades in the clear cold winter sky, it looks very eerie, almost ghost-like. It twinkles and sparkles like some visitor from another world. We discovered that the Druids held this constellation in high regard, and they actually considered it a collection of spirits from the other side. They believed that when the Pleiades was directly overhead at midnight, it was a time when our world and the spirit world came very close together and beings from the world of spirits were allowed to come into our plane of existence. This is known as the Druid holiday of Samhain and took place on the first day of November. Today we call the night before this holiday All Hallow's Eve, or Hallowe'en.

The belief that spirits from another plane of existence walked the earth at this time was carried through most of Europe into the Middle Ages and then carried over to the New World. People would dress up in costumes to convince these creatures that they were one of them and should be left alone. Many of these spirits were known to be very mischievous in nature and one had to leave tribute outside the door of their home to appease them. If a tribute was not left, then the demon would play a very nasty little trick on the house and the people who lived inside. This tribute in modern Halloween is known to us as "Trick or Treat." People would also place Jack-o'-lanterns outside their homes to show other spirits and demons that the house was already occupied by one of their kind and they should pass it to look for another home to possess.

The writing at the bottom of the stone was in Ogam which gave dedication to a high holiday and a warning that the chamber was on sacred ground. Later we would find another chamber less than two miles away with an identical stone, just over a meter in height, but it also showed the Seven Sisters clearly. As of the writing of this book, this chamber has been destroyed by the owner of the property, since he got tired of curious trespassers walking on his land. Also, the stone in the chamber on Route 301 vanished. There is no doubt that someone took it and now has it in their home as a showpiece or trophy. We received several letters from well-known psychics in the area warning us that the stone should be placed back where it was found, since it was a key that opened and closed a door to this other dimension of spirits.

Ancient Astronomers

We do know that the Druids were excellent astronomers. They plotted the motions of the planets and mapped the heavens. They were also able to predict lunar eclipses, solar eclipses, and the exact day of the equinoxes and solstices. Whoever built the chambers had a knowledge of astronomy since many of them are lined up with the rising and setting sun. We do know that a number of the very long gallery chambers were used to tell the change of seasons, very much like the long gallery chamber at Gungywamp.

One gallery chamber, which was used to tell the day of the Winter Solstice, is located in a wooded area in the town of Kent Cliffs. From the road it is about a one-mile walk through thick overgrowth and fallen trees. The chamber is one of three in that area, and one of the few that we found with a rock floor. What is remarkable about this chamber is that the rising sun shines directly through the door and strikes a flat rock on the back wall on the first day of winter. This was videotaped by researcher Enrique Noguera. During the experiment he also noticed that although the water just outside the chamber was frozen, the water inside the chamber was not. Many believe that the energy emitted from the chambers will cause this effect. During our research we did notice this in several chambers.

A Lunar-Planetary Conjunction

Fahnestock Park, a New York state park, is located in Putnam Valley close to the scenic Taconic Parkway. Most of the park is actually forest, and a favorite of hikers since it contains several hundred acres of trails. There are several chambers located in the park, two are intact and at least two have collapsed. The intact chambers are two of the most interesting we have investigated since there are a number of standing

stones around them and unusual mounds and ancient walls. In order
to reach the chamber locations you have to park in a somewhat hidden
turnoff which is actually the park ranger's entrance to that section of
the forest. If you follow the trail for about a half mile you will come to
three stones that have been carved, shaped, and placed in the ground.
Two stones have holes drilled in them, one of these has two holes that
go all the way through. The two holes are the width of the human eye
and if you look through them from the southern side the first chamber
is visible. If you look through the holes on the northern side there are
several overgrown mounds which look artificial.

A longtime resident of the area, and a frequent visitor to the park,
told Phil that the mounds are thought to be Indian burial grounds. The
standing stones have distinct shapes; two are almost square, while the
third is shaped like the head of some animal. Some say it looks like a
long-nosed lion, while others see a boar. Whatever they represent, they
were shaped, drilled, and placed in that location for a purpose. Behind
one of the standing stones is a flat rock that was placed in the ground
with a number of shapes carved in it. After chalking in the figures they
looked to us like a conjunction involving the moon and two bright
planets. Since the stone is orientated to the south, and the right side of
the moon is illuminated, we can assume that it is a evening conjunction. The two bright objects must be planets, judging from their size
and angle from the moon. They are, in our opinion, Jupiter and Venus.
Since we are dealing with the two brightest planets as seen from Earth
a conjunction of this type would have been a very important astronomical occurrence to ancient stargazers.

Our next step was to find out when a conjunction like this took
place. Using a computer with a planetarium program, we found out
that this configuration took place eight times in the last 3,000 years.
The dates were approximately 2492 B.C., 1965 B.C., 1164 B.C., 864 B.C.,
8 B.C., A.D. 300, A.D. 1431 and finally, A.D. 1952. The configuration
more resembled the 1965 B.C. and the 864 B.C. than any of the others.
The tree growth in that section of the park is recent and centuries ago
it was quite clear so they must have had a good view of the horizon.

An Ancient Settlement

Not far from Fahnestock Park we found a very interesting area that we called the "settlement" since it appeared as if someone a very long time ago attempted to start a small community. The dirt road that leads to the location is on private property and alongside the road are two chambers. The one on the bottom of the road is a gallery type and has a door which was placed there around 1953. This chamber also has a great deal of cement work in it and, according to the property owner, a gentleman in his early eighties, the chamber was used as a storage shed until 1967. He also told us that the chamber was there before his grandfather built the house in 1840. "No one really knows much about these things," He told us. "Some say they were built by the Druids thousands of years ago, some say they are just colonial root cellars. I believe they are much older than the colonial period and I'm happy that someone is trying to find answers as to where they came from." We stayed and listened to the elderly gentleman for almost an hour; he had a great deal of information about the township of Kent Cliffs since his family first settled there in 1760.

We then drove up the dirt road and came upon the second chamber. We noticed that the chamber actually went underground a few feet and the rocks of a once ancient wall were scattered to the left and right of the chamber. It seems that this was done when the road was constructed in the mid-1970s. We noticed that on the outside wall of the chamber was a triangular stone. We have seen similar stones in the same approximate locations on the outside front wall of a number of chambers. One thing that all these chambers had in common is that they were all oval or square in shape. The triangular stones all have three distinct sides indicating the three forces of nature that the Druids held sacred. We have also found standing stones with three slashes carved in them indicating the same thing. Many of these stones were always found within view of an oval chamber.

The idea of three was later translated into Christian beliefs with the Holy Trinity. Many other religions also hold the number three as being of divine origin. The magic number of three is also prominent in twentieth-century superstition; for example, "bad things always happen in threes."

The Eye of Bel

We then decided to split up and explore the land around the chamber. We stayed in touch by two-way radio and each of us explored opposite sides of the road. On both sides we found numerous carved stones that were laying in a ditch parallel to the road. There is no doubt that at one time these stones were standing up; they must have been knocked over when the road was widened. On the stones were a number of markings, but they were much too weathered to determine exactly what they were. Some looked like patterns of lines which if chalked in could have been the shapes of animal bodies, but they were just barely detectable from the natural scratches in the rock.

We also found a number of rock piles and something that looked like it could have been used as a small stone working bench or possibility an altar. As Phil explored the east side of the woods he came across a large flat-faced rock which looked like it had been placed in the Earth to point to the east. There was some type of markings on the rock and the oval pattern suggested that it was not natural. Phil then called for Marianne to come to his location and he began to chalk in the lines on the

rock. The pattern then became more distinct and began to look like an eye that was open. We were a little taken back because what we saw was something we only found in textbooks about archaeological Celtic finds in Brittany. It was the eye of Bel!

Bel was a Celtic god who was associated with fire and the arrival of

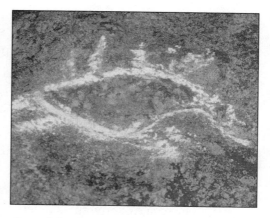

FIGURE 3.2 The Eye of Bel.

summer. The Celtic festival of Beltaine takes place on May 1, a day when the sun rises directly east. The belief in the god Bel can be traced back to ancient Phoenicia where the god was called Baal. After the Roman Empire converted to Christianity Bel and Baal, as with most of the old pagan gods, were identified as demons and fallen angels and worshipping them was considered evil. Bel and Baal were symbolized by an "all-seeing eye" and we wondered if the carved eye in the stone lined up with the rising sun on May 1. The festival of Beltaine was an important holy day since it marked the renewal of life and the warmth of the sun's energy returning to the northern hemisphere, today we call this holiday "May Day." Later, when we continued to do research on other deities, we found out the eye of Bel and Baal are very similar to the Egyptian "eye of Ra and Horus." The identification of Ra as a god associated with the sun predates Bel. Perhaps Ra was the first sun god worshiped, and the practice later carried to the people of the Middle East and the Celts.

Not far from the rock that had the eye of Bel inscribed in it was an oval rock with small holes drilled in it. The holes made up some type of pattern, and after a number of attempts trying to connect the holes, we finally realized that hole number 1 was on top and each successive hole to the bottom of the stone were 2, 3, 4, and so on. No two holes were at the same level, which made it easy. When we completed our work we saw an upside down "Y." Although to most people the pattern would not mean anything, to Phil it did.

The pattern inscribed on the rock was the constellation of Perseus. One star was highlighted in the pattern and it was in the exact position of the star Algol. Algol is Arabic for the "winking eye of the demon." Algol is an eclipsing binary star. This means that there are two stars in close proximity that orbit each other. From our view point on Earth, the double system appears as one star since they are very far from our planet. When the stars are alongside each other we see Algol at its brightest, when one star is behind the other, then we see it at its faintest. The change of brightness is very noticeable from Earth and its cycle from faint to bright is about 2.5 days. If some ancient astronomer observes this star over that time frame it would appear as if the star is blinking. Perhaps the Celts likened it to an eye opening and closing. We found many things at this location including a rock hidden in a shelter of stones which looks like a prehistoric ax head. We plan to go back and do a complete survey of this location to see what other hidden remnants of the Druids and Celts we could find.

CHAPTER 4

Enter, the Druids

WHO WERE THE DRUIDS? Where did they come from? Why did they have such an influence over the Celtic people? These are questions that had to be answered so that hopefully we could shed some light on the many mysteries that have unfolded. Julius Caesar is one of many important figures in history who had written about the Druids. He felt that the Druids came from southern Brittany, and then spread throughout Gaul. He wrote that the Druids had great honor among their people and they spent a great part of their lives accumulating more knowledge. The Druids generally settled all disputes, both public and private, for their people. They usually did not participate in war, nor did they have to pay taxes, but they had free use of all amenities.

The Druids also did not feel it proper to write their teachings down, although they used the Greek alphabet for public and private accounts. Caesar felt that there were two reasons why they did this: first, they did not want their ideas and beliefs published and second, they did not want those learning their beliefs to neglect the exercise of memory. Because of this two-fold practice, most of the great secrets of the Druids have been lost.

Their Position in Celtic Society

We discovered through continued research that the Celtic people who were part of this hierarchy made up three groups. The first level was a Bard, which took seven years of training. They were known for the composition of praise-poetry with the power of satire. The Bards had the ability through this medium to destroy a man's reputation. However, the evidence in our research had not uncovered any evidence of Bards in the New England area. The next level was a Vate and it took twelve years of training to reach this objective. The Vates—who were also called *seers*—had the power of prophecy and played a priestly part in sacrifices. At the end of the Druid reign, sacrifices took on a great significance in their religion. They were losing hold of the people to the Romans and Christianity, so the Vates oversaw the proper sacrifices to the gods.

The most prestigious position was that of a Druid, and it took nearly twenty years of study. Incidentally, although Druids were only priests, they were also doctors, lawyers, teachers, psychologists, philosophers, historians, prophets, astronomers, and political advisors. In short they were the intellectual class of the time. The many different Celtic tribes would seek out a Druid for guidance and advice since it was only through a Druid that the Celtic people could communicate with their gods.

Oak Doorways?

As we looked deeper into the origin of the Druids, we uncovered some very interesting information about the roots of the word. We found that the word "Druid" has a similar meaning in five different languages. In Gaelic the word *druidect* means "magic" and *druth* is "fool" or "madman," as in inspired madness. The word *dorus* means "door" and *druidim* is "to shut." In Sanskrit *drus* is "tree" and *doru* is "wood," in Lithuanian *derva* and *doire* are "oak," while *durys* is "door." This may infer if nothing else that the root from which Druid comes from is both widespread throughout the Indo-European world and had a powerful connection with oak trees and more importantly with the opening and closing of a spiritual door.

We found it fascinating that the word Druid had a connection with the opening and closing of "doors" since we suspected that our chambers may actually be portals to another dimension. We now knew more about what a Druid was, but where did they come from, what was their time frame in history? Could they be the ones responsible for building our mysterious stone chambers? We continued our research delving through as much material as we could get our hands on, and talking to anyone who knew anything about them. We found information that the Celtic people seem to have emerged in history somewhere near the headwaters of the Danube in western Germany. Herodotus, a writer who lived around 550 B.C., mentions them in connection with the source of the Danube, and Hecataeus, who lived somewhat later (circa 540–475 B.C.), mentioned a Celtic town called Nyrax that would be the modern-day equivalent to Styria in Austria. It is important to note that neither of these ancient writers seemed to be concerned with where the Celtic people actually were living at their time in history. It seems that the Greeks already knew quite a bit about them, since by 500 B.C. the Celts already appear to have been inhabiting a wide geographical area.

Pillars of Hercules

One other fascinating fact to note was that Herodotus mentions that the Celts lived beyond the Pillars of Hercules. Does this reference mean that the Celtic people had traveled past the Pillars of Hercules or that they came from past that point? This was a very interesting statement for us to find, since this would give evidence that they were already a seafaring people who traveled to the lands across the great ocean.

We found numerous references in a archaeological journal[1] that indicated that the region of the Upper Danube was the Celtic homeland from which these people had spread to Spain, France, and then later into Italy and the Balkans. A recognizably "proto-Celtic" culture was discovered to have existed around the upper Danube in 1000 B.C. However, some archaeologists now argue for a widespread and gradual "Celticization" of cultures that already existed in Bronze Age northern and western Europe. Thus, "Celtic" Brittany might date back as early as 1500 B.C.

Celtic Mother Goddess

The amount of effort and work that was needed to construct many of the stone chamber sites indicated to us that they were very important structures to the people who built them. This means that most likely some of them may have been used for some religious purpose. To get a better understanding of this we needed more information about the Celtic religion. The Celtic people worshiped a "Mother Goddess" named Danu. They had a female, maternal-based religion, which in turn gave the Celtic women equal rights in a time when most women were considered property. The name Danu means water from heaven, it is believed that the river Danube takes it name from her.

From myths about their gods we are told about the story of Danu watering the oak, which became the god Bel. Bel was considered the male fertility symbol and gave birth to the Dagda "the good god" who then fathered the rest of the gods. Bel was also known as the dispatcher of the dead, and it was his role to help the souls of dead Celts pass over to the other world. This may be why so many chambers in the Hudson Valley bear the three-slash Ogam that are the mark of Bel.

---

1 *Archaeology (Ireland)*, winter 1995 issue, volume 9, No. 4.

The Father of the Gods

Dagda, son of Danu and Bel, is father of nearly all the Irish gods and is also known by three other names making him a triune divinity. Many Celtic gods were worshiped in the triune, or triple, form. The concept of a three-personality god seems to have its roots in Indo-European expression. In Hindu belief, the Trimurti consisted of Brahma, the Creator; Vishnu, the Preserver; and Shiva, the Destroyer. The ancient Greeks saw the world ruled by three gods—Zeus (Heaven), Poseidon (Sea), Hades (Underworld). Three permeates Greek myth: the Fates are three, the Graces three, etc. In Christendom, the Holy Trinity is represented as the Father, Son, and Holy Ghost. The ancient Greeks, as well as the Celts, believed man was also a trinity composed of body, mind, and spirit. The world mankind inhabited is earth, sea, and air, and the divisions of nature are animal, vegetable, and mineral. To many ancient cultures three was the number of all things.

We began to understand the importance of the three slashes carved into the walls of many of the chambers. The Dagda appears as the patron of Irish Druidism. He is visualized as a man carrying a gigantic club, which he drags on wheels. One end can slay, while the other can heal. He has a black horse named Acein, or Ocean, and his cauldron, called Undri, is one of the major treasures brought from the city of Murias. It provides food so that no man went away from it hungry. It is the "cauldron" or "horn of plenty" which later generations of Christianized Celts developed into the Holy Grail of Arthurian myth. From this bit of history we can see how some part of one religion can be adopted into another to help people accept it.

After Christianity achieved its dominance in the Celtic world, legend says that the Celtic gods were forced to live in the hills—in the Irish language *sidhe* means mound or hill. Driven underground they became *aes sidhe*, people of the hills, or simply, fairies. Most famous of these fairies is the banshee (*bean sidhe*), the woman of myth whose wail and shriek portends a death. She is said to scream because she is shown a death and there is nothing she can do to stop it. We have been told numerous stories involving a chamber located on private property, the owners of which have been disturbed in the middle of the night by a noise that they could not identify. Did the portals open and allow a banshee wail to cross over into our world?

The Festivals of the Celtic Calendar

The Celtic calendar had thirteen months and nine seasonal festivals, which played a very important role in their civilization (see Appendix 2: Tables and Charts, page 135). The greatest festival in Ireland was known as *Samhain*. Samhain was also known as Hallowe'en, All Hallow's Eve, All Saints and All Souls' Day, and the Day of the Dead. It was celebrated on the first of November, but the night before was perhaps the most significant period of the festival, this part of the festival was called *Ruis*. Samhain took place on the thirteenth month and marked the end of the old year, and the beginning of the new one.

The evening before Samhain was the occasion in the year when the temporal world was thought to be overrun by the forces of magic. Magical troops issued from caves and mounds; men, too, could enter the Otherworld, but this was a hazardous undertaking. Monsters attacked people in their castles with flame and poison. At this time the gods moved freely in the world of humans and played cruel tricks on unsuspecting people. The chamber on Whangtown Road marks this festival and others with the morning sunrise. There are a number of rituals that mark this day, they include honoring ancestors, breaking old bad habits, foreseeing the future, and understanding death and rebirth.

The Winter Solstice also called *Alban Arthuan,* Yule, or Christmas, celebrated around December 22. The Celtic people believed that the energy involved at this time of the year was regenerating and renewing. The Celts followed a series of rituals that included personal renewal and the honoring of family and friends. The old Celtic yearly custom of gift-giving, singing, having a big feast, and lighting lights, is very similar to our Christmas.

Imbolc also called Candlemas and Brigid's Day, which is celebrated on February 1. It is recognized as a purification festival and was sometimes called "The Day of the Festival of the Bride." The goddess Brigid presides over this day and her festival coincided with the Christian feast of the purification of the Virgin Mary. In contrast to the Christian feast of the Virgin Mary, the eve of February 1, is also known as Candlemas eve.

The Vernal/Spring Equinox is celebrated on March 21, and also goes by the names *Alban Eiler,* St. Patrick's Day, and Easter. The Celtic people believed that the Earth energy which was strongest at this time of year to help new babies coming into this world. This included both human and animals births, as well as the sprouting of their crops. The rituals included days of fasting and meditation for spiritual enhancement, new growth, the starting of new projects, and the blessing of seeds that had been planted.

The next most important festival was held on May 1. This was the festival of *Beltaine,* also known as May Eve, May Day, and Walspurgis Night. England's Stonehenge lines up with the sun at certain times of the year, therefore we must assume that it must have been built for some solar cult. Beltaine means "the Fire of Bel" or "the Shining One" (the sun). Perhaps Stonehenge was used by the Celts to worship Bel on this day.

This was also a portentous time for the Celtic people. They had to make many sacrifices to ensure that their crops would be safe from blight and evil spirits. They would light two huge bonfires and drive the cattle herds between them to ensure their safety for the next year. All the Celtic festivals were in essence fire-festivals, and the Druids were very concerned with fire magic. The Druids believed that the souls of humans are immortal, and were located in the head rather than the chest. Fire and water were the two elements most revered and employed by the Druids in their sacred rites. Young animals were sacrificed at this fraught season, and there is some evidence for human sacrifice as well.

The Festival of *Alban Heruin* also called the Summer Solstice, Midsummer, or St. John's Day, and was celebrated on June 22. This was a time of the year when the Celts thanked the gods for their families and relationships. The rituals included the entire community, which would light bonfires with all-night vigils. There was also singing and feasting.

August 1 was called *Lughnasadh*. It also went by the names *Lughnassad* and *Lammas*. It was a feast in honor of the harvesting of crops, obviously a very important time of the year. The god of this festival was called Lugh who was also a potent patron of the Celtic arts and crafts as well as being worshiped by the ancient guild of cobblers. All that is left of this once mighty god are the legends that created the myth of the leprechaun, who was originally a fairy cobbler.

We had several reports of people seeing small beings that move quickly in and out of the chambers only to vanish. Is it possible that Lugh the ancient god of the Druids is visiting some of these places and making brief appearances, or are they leprechauns? Lugh had been the greatest of all the gods and the Dagda actually yielded to his commands. Later the Romans would replace the holiday and turn it into the Feast of Augustus, however the name still survives as Lunasa (August) in Irish.

The Autumn Equinox was also known as *Alban Elved,* Mabon, and Michaelmas. It was celebrated on September 23. The rituals that they followed during this time had to do with giving thanks for the abundance they had received, and introspection of the approaching winter. They followed customs that gave offerings to the land, bringing in the harvest and preparing for the upcoming cold weather, then finally the descent into darkness.

Ogma, the God of Eloquence

Ogma was god of eloquence and literature and a son of Dagda. He is credited with the invention of the Ogam script, named after him. His

parentage and adventures in many ways make him a comparative figure to Hercules, who was the son of Zeus, father of the Greek gods.
Ogam can be traced back to the fourth century A.D. and possibly as far
back as 500 B.C., and is better suited as a sign language, which would
make sense since the Druids did not believe in writing things down.

Another piece of the puzzle that we uncovered was that a major
underlying theme in the Druids ideology was that burials represent a
belief that death is a transitional period (not an event) intervening
between this world and the Otherworld. During this period the body
and the soul are formless and stateless. This period is terminated with
a formal ceremony marking the arrival of the soul in the next world.
This statement was to make more sense after a talk with one of our
psychic colleagues, Loretta. (Loretta's comments can be found in chapter 6, "Mysteries of Ninham Mountain.")

An article in *Archeology Today* states that cremations were a normal
funeral rite in certain parts of England during the time of the Celts.[2]
These cremated remains were frequently furnished with grave goods,
the most frequent being a single urn derived from a restricted range of
beakers or similar vessels. This brought us back to story that was told to
us at Gungywamp when the sealed chamber was opened and a single
urn was found sitting in the middle of the floor which contained mysterious remains. The urn was taken in for testing, but the archeology
department misplaced it. Was the evidence covered up on purpose?
Perhaps archaeologists are not ready to accept new theories and the urn
was lost in the basement of the university because it did not fit in with
current theory. We now had a better understanding on who the Celts
and the Druids were, the next task was to find evidence of their existence in ancient America.

---

2 *Archaeology Today (Ireland)*, winter 1995 issue, volume 9, No. 4.

CHAPTER 5

America's Stonehenge

THERE WERE QUITE A few chambers to study in New York, but it was important at this time to take a look at similar megalithic structures in New England. For years we heard about chambers and standing stones found in Vermont, New Hampshire, and Massachusetts. As you proceed north, the chambers in New York become more sparse in the town of Fishkill, which is located in Dutchess county. No chambers are found between northern Dutchess county and southern Massachusetts. The stone chambers once again appear in southern Massachusetts, Vermont, and New Hampshire. We knew that it was vital to our research to visit these locations and compare similarities with the stone chambers in the Hudson River Valley of New York.

On August 3, 1996, we planned a three-day trip to visit some of these locations to collect enough information for our research. We planned to go four different locations. The first was the town of Shutesbury, Massachusetts, where we read about small chambers that were rumored to have been built by Irish monks sometime in the seventh century A.D. Our next stop was to be a complex of stone megaliths that was known as "America's Stonehenge," or "Mystery Hill," in North Salem, New Hampshire. We also planned to investigate a number of chambers in Woodstock, Vermont, and finally end our trip investigating a recent megalithic find in—coincidentally enough—Woodstock, New York.

The "Monk's Caves"

We arrived in Shutesbury, Massachusetts during the late afternoon and although we had directions we had no idea where to find the "Monk's Caves." This was totally understandable, because we were not familiar with the area. People looking for chambers in the Hudson Valley have the same trouble and will drive right by one on the side of the road. We knew we would have difficulty so we began to look for assistance. We stopped at the Shutesbury Town Historic Museum, but since it was Saturday they were open by appointment only. A woman across the street directed us into town and suggested we try the post office. As we drove into the town we looked for anyone who could help us, but the town seemed to be shut down for the weekend. Luckily, the post office

FIGURE 5.1 Site of Monk's Cave, Shutesbury, Massachusetts.

was still open and a woman there knew a gentleman who lived very near the location. She called the man on the telephone and arranged for us to meet him. She then showed us a map and instructed us on how to get to his home. We arrived at his home fifteen minutes later and he showed us the location of not only the "Monk's Cave," but also the location of a second one.

We drove down the road that he directed us, stopped the car, got out and packed up our equipment to begin our search for the "cave." We began walking and it wasn't long before we spotted our objective. It was located right along the side of the road that led to a Buddhist retreat. It turned out we were lucky to come from that particular direction since if we had approached it from the other side, we would have missed it.

This structure was very different from the chambers in the Hudson Valley. The entrance looked like it had been carved right out of the side of the hill. The builders seemed to have just hollowed out an area and then supported it with stones in a similar, but somewhat different, fashion than the New York chambers. It seems to us that this particular chamber was designed for protection from the elements, and to perhaps hide from hostile natives. The chamber was much smaller than anything else we had seen before. It was circular in shape and had a single, thick, large capstone for a roof supported by the walls. We found three slashes on a rock just outside the chamber that looked like Ogam writing. As of the writing of this book we have yet to have these ideographs interpreted. However, the three slashes in the fashion that we saw are indications that whoever built this particular so-called "Monk's Cave" may have been giving dedication to the Celtic god Bel. If they were early Christian Irish monks, what were they doing dedicating the chamber to Bel? According to early Christian beliefs this would have been a sacrilege. Perhaps the builders were not Irish monks, but other later Celtic people who journeyed to the New World.

After packing up our gear, we took a side trip to the Buddhist retreat, Temenos, to see if any one there knew anything about the local "caves." It was a very peaceful place, however, no one was there at that time. There were quite a number of carved monoliths in the area, but one in particular had a fascinating story. No one knows who carved it, but it has been speculated to be the work of Irish monks during the tenth century. The actual carving looks very reminiscent of Cernunnos, a Celtic god who appears in the Gundestrup cauldron in Denmark. It is shaped much like the ones used by Christian monks in Ireland and the people at Temenos feel there may be a connection with the "Monk's Caves."

We finally located a woman who seemed to be caretaker of the retreat. She was filling water bottles from a well. She took the time to speak with us and said that the people who founded the retreat picked this location because of the high energy in the area. We found this quite interesting since in the town of Kent Cliffs, New York, there is a Buddhist monastery. When we asked the headmaster why they picked this location to build the monastery he replied, "Because the energy is strong here." Coincidentally enough, this area in Kent Cliffs, New York, also has the greatest number of stone chambers in all of New York state, and is the center of the UFO activity in the Hudson Valley.

After Temenos we continued on our journey to locate the other "Monk's Cave." This time we felt it would be beneficial to split up and use our walkie-talkies to communicate since we had to hike quite a distance from the road and were not sure of the location of the chamber. After a considerable time searching, Marianne called to Phil to tell him that she had found it. He joined her at the location and we noticed that this "cave" was almost identical to the first one we had found. The tiny chamber was designed in such a way that if one was walking by it one would think that it was just a dirt mound with a hole in it. It was apparent that both "caves" were constructed about the same time by the same people since they were almost identical. We took accurate measurements of both chambers and these are given below (all dimensions are given in inches).

	Chamber One:	Chamber Two:
Height:	70	62
Width:	76	64
Length:	65	60
Door Height:	29	28
Width:	29	18
Opening:	East	South

America's Stonehenge

Our next stop was America's Stonehenge. Our previous research had
told us that this is one of the largest and possibly the oldest megalithic
(stone-constructed) sites in North America. It has puzzled archaeologists, astronomers, and historians for decades. "The site was opened to
the general public in 1958 by Mr. Robert E. Stone of Derry, New Hampshire, for the purpose of public education, research and preservation.
Since that date research has been conducted on many fronts, the most
exciting and conclusive of which has been the recognition of the many
astronomical alignments, making it one of North America's oldest and
largest calendrical site. The complex, which covers over thirty acres, is
series of stone walls containing large carved standing stones, several
chambers, and a number of monoliths that have definite astronomical
alignments. The majority of these standing stones can still be used to
determine specific solar and lunar events."

Excavation at the site "has uncovered numerous historic and pre-his-
toric artifacts such as, stone tools, pottery, and carbon samples suitable
for radiocarbon dating. Charcoal from two of these excavations in 1969
and 1971 proved to be 3,000 and 4,000 years old respectively."[1] Just
from this information alone we can be sure of one thing: this site was
built by people who were here long before Columbus sailed into the
new world. At the very least, it is most likely the oldest man-made construction in the United States, a giant megalithic astronomical complex
constructed some time during the Bronze Age.

Armed with this information we were very excited to actually see the
complex. We had an early start that day and arrived in the morning. We
entered the visitor center building that housed a small museum. We
took a good look around, purchased our tickets, and headed in to see
the wonders. The first chamber we saw has been named the "Watch
House" because of its location outside of the main complex area. It is a
beautiful chamber that uses a glacial boulder on one side which seems

---

1 America's Stonehenge web site.

to have used to shelter the chamber. Unlike the chambers in the Hudson Valley which have from five to seven stones that make up the ceiling, this chamber has one large one capstone that was more cylindrical in shape. However, the similarity with the Hudson Valley chambers is that both have openings toward a southeasterly direction. As we left this chamber we realized we were at one end of a doubled-walled pathway, we followed it and saw that it lead to the main site, which contained a series of complex stone walls. Many of these walls contained stone slabs that had been placed in an upright position. This placement of stones is uncommon in New England colonial wall construction and is thought to have been built at the same time as the rest of the complex. We proceeded to enter the central complex and were quite overwhelmed by what we saw. There were so many walls, markings, and stone megaliths that we really didn't know where to start. Although we spent the entire day there and did a considerable amount of research this chapter only permits us space enough to cover the main points of the complex.

We proceeded on a pathway that lead to a very fascinating area called the "Oracle Chamber." Approaching the chamber, we found a familiar V-shaped groove in the stone that was very similar to the way rocks were cut in ancient Europe using a hand drill. As we entered the Oracle Chamber we immediately realized that this was like no other chamber in the Hudson Valley. The Oracle Chamber is much more complex; it was not just a single room going straight back, but a number of rooms all tied together.

As we walked into the main entrance, we entered a room that was conical in shape. We noticed that the walls were very straight with no corbelling and the corners were constructed at very sharp angles. To our left there was an opening large enough for a person to crawl into and be completely hidden. This person could then observe almost all activity in the chamber through a small opening near the floor. At the far end of the main room was an opening in the roof that looked like it may have been used as a chimney. Near the back of the wall, on the right side were a number of unusual marks carved into the rock. They looked like a horseshoe, with the opening pointing down to the floor.

Although the actual meaning of these symbols is still unknown to us, many cultures regarded similar signs as good luck. The two points of the symbol had to be pointed downward since these cultures believed that this would ward against evil. One example of this is the pentagram. When the two points of the pentagram are pointed downward, it is said to keep evil away; however, if the two points are facing upward the sign works in reverse and attracts evil and bad luck. Off to the right was a second room in which the builders had used a piece of bedrock for one of the supporting walls. Running along the entire length of the wall was a stone bench that had been apparently carved right out of the bedrock. We were amazed to see a carving on the wall that looked very much like a running deer or an ibex. We closely examined a underground drainage system that seemed to be designed to drain water from the chamber. Getting down on our hands and knees to get a better look we were able to shine our flashlight quite some distance back into the earth. Whoever built this system did an excellent job since it was designed to drain off large volumes of water from the chamber during flooding rains. We were able to walk out of the chamber at the back of the second room. This was not part of the original structure, and we were told that vandals had broken through at this location and later the visitor center decided to use it as an exit for tours.

We walked around outside to the back of the Oracle Chamber to take a look at what has been called the "Sacrificial Table." It is a 4.5-ton grooved slab that was believed to have been used for sacrifices. It is roughly the size of a person, and has a carved channel running along the edge of it with a drain located on the lower corner, which is tilted. It was thought that these drains were used to channel off blood. The table has a secret tunnel below it that is attached to the Oracle Chamber. This tunnel may have used as a speaking tube which gave the impression that the table was talking. Because of this secret tube and hidden room within the chamber archaeologists named it the "Oracle Chamber."

As we left the Sacrificial Table we walked up to a raised viewing area and from here we were able to see the astronomical stones lined up with

Figure 5.2 North Pole Star Monolith, America's Stonehenge, New
Hampshire.

the cardinal points of the compass. In the immediate area there were also
several other standing stones, also cut with precision. Researchers in the
late 1950s discovered that they are aligned with the rising and setting sun
during the solstices, equinoxes, and perhaps were also used to predict
lunar and solar eclipses. The stones are set in the earth in a radiating circle from a central point so we took the main path which passed by each
of these monoliths to get a better look at them.

The Winter Solstice Sunset Monolith was the first stone suspected to
have solar alignment. This stone marked the most southerly point of
the setting sun almost 4,000 years ago, but is off today because of a
slight change in the direction that the Earth points to in space. This
wobbling of the Earth's orbit is called "precession of the equinox," and
is the reason why every several thousand years we have a "new" North
Star. If our readers are more interested in finding out more about this

orbital phenomenon, we suggest that you look up the information in any basic astronomy book.

Our next stop was the Summer Solstice Sunset Monolith and because of the way it was carved it turned out to be one of our favorites. This stone marked the most northerly setting of the sun at this latitude approximately 4,000 years ago. As we proceeded on the northeast section of the trail we came upon another stone that marked the position of true north and from our calculations it still had a close alignment with Polaris, the pole star. On our walk we saw some other interesting low walls and some stones that appeared to have been carved into the shapes of animals. Due to the limited space we will not be able to go into full detail of all the wondrous things we saw. If you are in the New Hampshire area and are interested in the subject, we highly recommend that you visit Mystery Hill because it is truly the "Stonehenge of North America."

When we finished the day we were exhausted, so we retired to our hotel here we talked about all the things we had discovered. The chambers at America's Stonehenge were certainly built in a different manner than the ones in the Hudson Valley. This gave us more evidence that the chambers in New York and New England were much older than anyone previously thought and were built by many different cultures.

The next morning we had to make a quick decision, because the time we had spent at America's Stonehenge was greater than what we had allowed for, so we had to make a choice between the Vermont stop or go straight to the chambers at Woodstock, New York. Since we had an appointment with someone to show us the locations in New York, we thought it would be best to forego the Vermont chambers. We drove most of the morning to reach Woodstock, and finally arrived at the home of our guide.

CHAPTER 6

Mysteries of Ninham Mountain

NINHAM MOUNTAIN IS THE highest point in Putnam County, New York. From its peak, which rises over 1,600 feet above sea level, you can see most of Putnam, Westchester, and Dutchess counties of New York. It is a domed mountain composed of many granites and a great number of minerals, including quartz, feldspar, garnet, mica, and magnetite. Since it is the highest point in the area, the state police and federal government have built an antenna "farm" on top of the mountain, so communications for all law enforcement agencies can be carried out throughout the southern part of New York. Also atop the mountain is a ranger tower over 100 feet high. The view from the tower is truly amazing, and the entire Hudson River Valley can be seen from this vantage point.

First Encounter

Phil first became aware of Ninham Mountain around 1984, during the early days of investigating the UFO sightings in the Hudson River Valley. His investigation team was looking for a high vantage point to set up cameras and radio equipment to try and document some of the sightings taking place. A resident of Putnam County contacted Phil and told him about the ranger tower on top of the mountain and how it would be a great spot to set up an observation post since he would be able to keep several counties under surveillance.

The first time Phil arrived at Ninham mountain was in July of 1985. He was able to drive his car about halfway up the mountain road but then had to park the car and walk since the rest of the road became a winding dirt trail that cut into a heavily overgrown area. As he continued up the mountain he began to notice a stone wall to his right that ended in a small clearing. He noticed what looked like a mound of stones covered by thick vines and shrubs. He then took a closer look and realized it was a chamber that was hidden by the overgrowth for what seemed like a very long time. He cleared away the vines and confirmed that it was indeed another stone chamber (Figure 6.1, below).

FIGURE 6.1 Chamber at Ninham Mountain, New York.

This was the sixth time he came across a chamber in relation to a location that was known to have a great deal of paranormal reports, especially UFO sightings. However, the main task that day was to make his way to the top of the mountain and climb the tower and try to document anything unusual that night in the sky. Since it was beginning to get dark he left the mystery of the chamber for another day, and proceeded to his destination.

Phil reached the top of the mountain at sunset and began to climb the 100-foot tower. The view was fantastic! At about midnight it started to get very breezy and the tower actually swayed back and forth. Although it was July, the windchill at the top was a mere 35 degrees Fahrenheit. He saw nothing strange in the sky that night, however something was taking place on the ground below, unknown to Phil at that time.

At 2:00 A.M. he climbed down the stairs of the tower, and began walking down the dark mountain path to where the car was parked. He felt a little strange and very uneasy, it was as if someone was watching him. He thought to himself, "Well, this is how one of those bizarre horror movies start, some idiot walking in the woods in an isolated area in the middle of the night when all of a sudden some psycho comes out with a chainsaw or some prehistoric beast that has been sleeping for a million years decides to wake up and have dinner."

Although no strange creatures appeared out of the woods, there was some type of activity going on. Phil heard a strange buzzing sound followed by a crack. This repeated over and over again at an interval of about fifteen seconds. The crack sounded as if someone was walking in the woods and stepping on a twig. Phil stopped at the location of the chamber and saw what appeared to be flashes of light close to the ground on the right side of the trail, perhaps 200 yards in the woods. As he watched, the same thing appeared on the left side of the trail at about the same distance. The activity looked like the light of a camera flash, yet the strange thing was that the flashes on the right were blue-white, while the flashes on the left were yellow. The lights were about as bright as lightning flashes and, according to Phil's observations, they looked like some type of electrical or plasma discharge.

As Phil walked into the woods he could never seem to get close enough to the flashes. It was if they moved further away from him every time he tried to close in on the source. Perhaps the source was actually a great deal further away, and if this was the case the amount of energy needed to produce such an energy burst was enormous. The flashes did not seem to radiate from one particular point, but appeared to come from all directions. Every time a flash took place, the trees would light up and the dark trail was illuminated. Phil decided to return to the trail, as he was walking he began to feel very lightheaded and dizzy. He stopped and sat on a rock for several minutes and then the flashes of light slowly faded and vanished. When the flashes vanished, he felt fine and got up and walked to the car and went home mystified about the events of the night. For weeks Phil was excited about what took place and decided to do research on the history of the mountain and the geology of the area.

The Medicine Man

The mountain itself was formed by upward pressure of magma about 125 million years ago. Metals like iron ore, in the form of magnetite, melted due to great pressure and was forced to the surface of the earth. Other minerals like quartz, feldspar, garnet, and malachite along with intrusive granite also worked their way to the surface. For centuries, the base of the mountain was the home of the Wappinger tribe, who were part of the Mohegan and Delaware tribes. The mountain was named by the colonial settlers after Daniel Ninham, the last sachem, or great chief, of the Wappinger tribe. The mountain was held sacred by the Indians for many years and only a high chief or a medicine man (or his student) were allowed to venture to the top. A medicine man would instruct his student that he must venture to the top of the mountain and fast there for three days until he had a vision of the ancient ones from the spirit world. The Wappinger believed that at the peak of the mountain was a gateway to another world. They thought that at certain times of the year, if the conditions were right, it would be possible for a holy man to communicate with this other world and perhaps venture into it.

During our investigation, Phil was introduced to a ninety-year old or older medicine man, the last of his kind. In 1991, Phil went to study with him for three weeks and gathered information not only about Ninham Mountain, but also the chambers. To protect his identity we will not use his English name, but his Indian name, "Onawani Tu," which, in English means, "He who walks with the spirits," or Spirit Walker. So we shall refer to him simply as Spirit Walker.

Before Spirit Walker even began to talk with Phil, he asked: "Do you believe in the old ways?" Phil answered "yes" and Spirit Walker said to him, "I will teach you, but you must ask me questions, because I will not be around very much longer." He told Phil the legend about the mountain and the people who lived there a very long time ago. Spirit Walker told of his experience at the top of the mountain when he was sent there as a young boy by his teacher as training to become a medicine man. Phil then asked him about the chambers and his experiences at Ninham Mountain. These experiences are presented as follows. Some of the information has been left out, because he was told things about Indian mysticism that he promised to keep secret, and to only pass on to a worthy student when the time was right.

The Voice of Mother Earth

When I was a boy, I was taken to the base of the mountain by a very old wise man. Although most of us were only part Indian, we were still accepted as their own by the full-blooded members of the tribe. We lived with the white people in the area, but often kept our heritage and ideas to ourselves. The old wise man was a medicine man and there were three of us, but only one would be selected that day to take his place. I don't remember the year exactly, but it must have been around 1910. He took us to the base of the mountain and showed us the chamber and the stones that were behind it. He told us that a long time ago no one was allowed past the point of the chamber unless you were a sachem or a powerful medicine man. He said that although the spirits are still present they are much weaker than they were centuries ago.

He then took us over to one of the great stones that was standing up and asked us to put our hands on it and place our ear against it one at a time. With each boy he asked, "What do you hear?" The first boy said nothing, then I tried and he asked once again, "What do you hear?" I then heard a humming sound that almost sounded like a musical instrument, it pulsated. I then took my hands off the rock, and it stopped. I told him what I heard and he smiled and said, "You are gifted, you are chosen for you can hear Mother Earth sing." The other boy then ran to the stone and tried to listen, but he heard nothing. He then dismissed the other two and sent them home. The wise man then sat me down and began to tell me the story about the stones and the people who put them there.

Spirit Walker then grew tired and told Phil that he would continue the story the next day. Phil retired to his room and contemplated what he had been told that day. What did he mean by "Mother Earth singing?" As Phil thought about it more deeply he realized that he had seen the stones that Spirit Walker was talking about. Although the huge carved stone is no longer standing, it was once imbedded in quartz bedrock and the stone itself has considerable veins of quartzite running through it.

If energy did come from the Earth, and was focused at Ninham, then it could be generated through the quartz and produce a resonating effect. We do the same thing today with radio transmitters and computer chips. We cut quartz crystals to a certain shape and thickness and run an electric current through them, the result is an energy wave used to operate our computers and communication equipment. The mountain generated some sort of energy that at one time must have been focused through the standing stones, but now from what Phil saw that summer night on the mountain, it seemed no longer focused.

We read about similar experiences at Stonehenge in England. Some people would walk up to the stones and feel a vibrating energy or hear a hum, but most people would not experience anything. Perhaps it was because some people are more empathic than others and their nervous systems are more sensitive. We do know from history that the best healers are those who can feel their patient's pain; in other words, a psychic.

We also know that animals can sense changes in magnetic fields since it is a documented fact that dogs, cats, cattle, and birds (just to name a few) seem very uneasy before a major earthquake. For years this was not understood, then it was found that the pressure in the rock just before an earthquake is great. The pressures on the rock containing a number of different minerals, including quartz, will cause great tensional energy. The quartz and other crystals resonate and send out an energy wave, which is picked up by animals and sensitive people. Also, in earthquake areas people have reported strange globes of light or flashes. This energy is being generated by the pressure on the crystals in the rock, and is called *piezoelectric* energy or current.

The Faces of Fire

The next day Phil awoke early and met with Spirit Walker and asked him to tell the story of the stone chambers as promised. "Before we begin," Spirit Walker replied, "come with me." Phil then went outside and on the ground he saw a stone medicine wheel. He was asked, "First touch the southern stones." Phil touched the stones and, to his surprise, in spite of the sun hitting them, they felt very cold. Then he was told, "Now go to the stones facing north and touch them." Phil touched the northern stones and was once again surprised to find that they were very warm, almost hot. Spirit Walker then said, "Before I tell you the story you must see that energy whether it be from Mother Earth or from all living creatures can be stored and then used once again. This medicine wheel directs and centers my life force and all positive energy in this area is focused through it. It protects this sacred area (he then pointed to mounds in the distance) where others who came before me rest. The stones you are interested in store energy." Then he began to tell of the Indian legend of the stone chambers.

A very long time ago, much longer than the trees remember, my people lived in prosperity and in peace. Then one day the strange men came from across the sea from the direction of the rising sun. The ships came and they were very long, with eighteen to each ship. These men, their faces were of fire (red beards) and their eyes were of the sky (blue eyes). They were much larger than my people and had fur on their bodies and horns out of their heads[1] (fur clothes and armor with helmets). My people greeted them as friends and they began to build the stone huts that you call the chambers. It is said that the stones were moved by spirit power with a great wind (this was an interesting comment since according to legend the megaliths at Stonehenge were moved to their present location by a whirlwind created by Merlin).

At night it was said that they would light great fires and circle the stones, then spirits would appear and take form. These people were considered by us to be the messengers of the Great Spirit; they lived with my ancestors for a very long time. There was a great exchange of ideas and knowledge with not only our tribe, but also with the Delaware, Algonkian, and the Huron people. Then one day they were gone, but my people still held the mountain that they lived on to be sacred and a place where the spirit world and our world comes together.

After a short rest, Phil then asked him of his experiences at the mountain and the training he went through to become a medicine man. This story follows.

The Vision Quest

When I was a boy and ready to begin my training as a medicine man, I was told that I would be the last of my kind. I was then instructed to climb the north slope of the mountain; here I was to fast and meditate for three days. This was my vision quest, but first I had to purify my body and mind so that I could talk with the spirits to find the answer to the great mystery. I climbed the mountain and it was a very hot day in the summer. By the time I reached the peak I was thirsty and tired, but I was not allowed to drink or eat anything for a period of three days. I walked over to the sacred area and began to chant. I stayed

---

1   It is known that Celts wore horned helmets; the Vikings wore helmets with wings.

there for two days and two nights and nothing took place. I was almost ready to give up and go home because I was hungry and thirsty. I then heard the voice of my teacher in my head telling me that my faith would be tested and I must continue to endure a short time longer.

The next day passed quickly and as the third night fell the moon was full and the wind became strong. I was very cold, but I did not move from my position. I felt no more pain and discomfort and my mind and thoughts were almost separated from my body. I then heard a rumbling sound and opened my eyes because I thought a storm was coming—it sounded just like thunder in the distance, but there was not a cloud in sight. Then I began to feel that ants were crawling over my body, my hair, which was very long at that time, began to stand up and I could feel waves of tingling up and down my spine. As I listened to the rumbling, it then sounded almost like voices and then the voices got clearer, but I still could not understand what the words were. The words sounded like the language that I heard the old ones in the tribe speak during a ceremony. I then looked up and over my head and saw that a white cloud started appearing out of nowhere. The cloud grew over my head and it was like the cloud was being pushed into our world from an invisible tunnel. Then seven globes of light came out of the cloud. All seven of them were different colors. I remember yellow, red, blue, amber, white, green, and a very bright orange. The lights were beautiful to look upon and I was not scared. I felt at peace.

The lights then circled the mountain for a short time and then came down and formed a circle around me. They stood about a man's height above the ground and all of them began to get brighter and then dim (pulsate). Then as I watched they all at once began to take shape, the shape of a human being. I could not see their features fully because the glow from each of them was so bright. I could tell that they were all women from their forms. I could also tell that they had deep eyes and were all smiling at me. They were all very beautiful with very long hair the color of silk and as white as the snow. I wanted to get up and walk to one of them and touch them, but before I could move I heard a voice say, "Do not move, you cannot touch us, it is not permitted, for we are of two worlds." Then without warning I felt as if I was falling backward. The next thing I knew I was out of my body. I could see myself still sitting there, at first I thought my body was dead, but was relived to see that it was still breathing. Then I realized that my body was just a shell and that what I was now was the real me. I felt no more cold, thirst, or hunger.

The spirits were now gone, but I then heard one of them say that now I must fulfill my destiny. I was now in spirit and walked down the mountain. I wanted to leave the mountain so I started to float into the air, then, right in front of me a tunnel opened up and I was drawn in to it. The tunnel was short and I emerged in this village and there was a home with a woman crying outside. I walked by a number of people and they didn't see me. I walked into the home and there was this young boy lying on a bed dying. I walked over to him and he saw me and smiled. I knew what to do, I extended my arms over his body and a yellow light came out and covered him. The next thing I knew I was back in my body up at the mountain. I was very weak and tired. I tried to stand up, but collapsed. I blacked out for an unknown amount of time and when I woke I was home in my bed with my mother and my teacher looking over me smiling. He told me that I met with the spirits and now could finish learning the higher mysteries that he would teach me. Two weeks later my teacher took me to the nearby villages to introduce me. He brought me to a settlement in north Litchfield County, in Connecticut, and as I walked from the horse carriage I saw the boy I had healed in my vision. He ran up to me and yelled, "Mother this is the spirit boy who came and healed me." I was happy to hear that because now I was sure that what took place was not some kind of dream induced from lack of food and rest, but a real experience.

The Wisdom of the Animal Spirit

The story was truly amazing to say the least, but there was doubt in Phil's mind and Spirit Walker knew this. Being trained as a scientist, he was skeptical and asked, "Do you have the ability to leave your body at any time?" Spirit Walked answered, "Yes." Phil was then told to go into the next room and, when given the word, to start holding up fingers and pick up items. He was told by Spirit Walker that he would leave his body, and enter the room with him, but he would stay connected to his body partially so that he could talk. Phil entered the next room and started picking up items and also held fingers in the air, to his surprise Spirit Walker was able to identify each item or number.

Later that evening Phil was taught how the Native Americans designed peace pipes, bows, and other tools used in ceremonies. All the objects have a connection with the earth, sky, elements, and spirits. It was clear that a great deal of the Wappinger and Algonkian beliefs came from the people who built the stone chambers and erected the standing stones. In the following days, Phil was shown his spirit animal and how to communicate with it. He was also given more information about the structures on the mountain, especially a very interesting area behind the chamber on the main trail.

The Ritual Area

Located about thirty yards behind the Ninham chamber is a cleared area with a very old wall surrounding it. At one time the wall enclosed the location, but when the road was put in part of the wall that extended across the path was destroyed. The wall is truly an amazing sight. It is made of iron ore plus a great deal of quartzite. On the wall one can find many markings and carvings that look like animal shapes. The wall seems to enclose what appears to be some type of ancient ritual area. The bedrock has been elevated and shaped to look like a stage. On top of the stage are two quartzite platforms that were taken out of the nearby outcropping of the mineral and placed on top of the stage. A closer examination of this pure solid quartz revealed several ancient drill marks. On top of these platforms are oil marks which have been soaked into the mineral, perhaps these blocks of quartz were used to hold oil fires. The most remarkable find is located on the west side of the stage, an altar made out of pure quartz. The altar is the length and width of a man and it looks like a body could have been placed on it during some type of ceremony.

It is our belief from researching the Druid rituals that a body may have been placed in the chamber and then on the altar where it was prepared for burial, or sometimes burned. The altar does look as if there had been several hot fires around it, since carbon can be seen etched into the quartz, discoloring it. On several occasions, people lay-ing on the altar have reported becoming dizzy; some even claim to have heard voices, or have had visions.

On November 1, 1996, we brought a few friends to Ninham Moun-tain and decided to camp out near the ritual and chamber area. It was the coldest night of the year so far and although nothing really took place, one member of our party reported hearing strange voices on his radio, voices speaking in a language he could not understand. Also, two psychics who were with us reported that they felt the presence of interdimensional beings, but nothing manifested that night.

In the weeks to follow, we took infrared photographs of the chamber area at night and got a number of streaks of light that seemed to emanate from the opening of the chamber. Although the images were quite bright on film, we could see nothing with our eyes. A French sci-entist[2] once proposed the theory that a great deal of paranormal phe-nomena is invisible to us because it radiates energy in the infrared part of the spectrum, which cannot be seen by the human eye.

UFO Encounters

Ninham Mountain has a history of UFO sightings. Strange lights have been seen on many occasions circling the mountain, and some wit-nesses have even reported large clusters of lights settling down on its summit. A restaurant owner in the area reported to us that during many nights she saw globes of brilliant lights of various colors circle the mountain. The description of these lights is almost identical to what the Indian medicine man experienced eighty years or so ago.

Perhaps the most interesting close encounter with the spirit lights of Ninham was of a forty-eight-year old male who often hunted and camped on the mountain. He told us his story in 1992, and it follows. Since he is an ex-intelligence officer with a secret government agency, we will have to refer to him as Thatcher.

---

2   Dr. Jon-Marie Marres of the University of Paris, 1989 paper on infrared radiation.

Saved from a Frozen Death

I was up at Ninham Mountain in January, 1990, and I was doing a little hunting and just walking through the woods. I reached the top of the mountain and the wind was really gusting hard. I bet the wind-chill factor was at least 40 below zero. I was walking through the woods on the north side of the forest when it started to snow. I was already very cold and with the sun gone the temperature began to drop. The wind also started to gust and I could feel my hands, feet, and face starting to develop frostbite.

It then began snowing so hard that I could not see ten feet in front of me. I was then lost and could barely move. I was pretty high up and there was nothing really to shelter me from the wind since most of the trees were bare. The sky was very dark and there was a fog all around me, the fog was so thick that it was difficult to see and I started to lose my orientation as to what direction I was heading. I then felt dizzy and fell and I couldn't move. I thought to myself that this was it, someone will find me weeks from now frozen to death. I then felt no pain and I knew this was a bad sign. I looked up to the sky and my face started to get covered with snow. I could not move—it was as if all my joints were frozen solid. As I looked up to the sky, right overhead ten or more lights of different colors appeared out of nowhere and started to come down. I heard no sound and the lights were in the shape of a circle. It was a very strange thing to see because they looked very fuzzy through the mist and fog. Then I blacked out.

The next thing I remember I woke up in the ranger's station. He told me that he found me at the bottom of the parking area lying down on top of the hood of my car. He also said that he received a telephone call saying I was there. I don't know how I got there since there was no way that I could have walked all that distance on my own. Those lights must have been some sort of ship, maybe a UFO. They must have been friendly since they saved me from being frozen. It seems that from the point that I blacked out to the time that I woke up in the ranger's house was about forty minutes of time, so it's not like I was missing for days. Whoever they were they didn't keep me in their ship for a long period of time. The only thing I remember is being in a room and see-ing canisters with figures that looked like people in them. I know this sounds a little crazy, but in the dream I think I remember seeing a can-ister that was empty and I really feel that whoever they were they are going to come back for me because that's the canister that I'm supposed to be in.

Thatcher had a UFO experience of some type and was transported off the mountain by some unknown intelligence. This intelligence also may have made the call to the ranger so that he could be rescued. What are the lights of Ninham Mountain? Are they some alien intelligence, or are they the spirits that guard and protect the mountain?

The Spirit of Daniel Ninham

As mentioned earlier, the mountain was named after the last great sachem of the Wappinger, Daniel Ninham. We do know that Chief Ninham tried to protect his land from colonial settlers, but even his great influence and power could not stop the changing of the times. He thought that if he took his braves and went to war against the French for the English, then the King of England would grant his request that his homeland be preserved for his people for all time. Daniel did in fact take his braves to war, but all were killed in the first battle and as the years went by the sacred land of the Wappinger was lost to the white man. It is still said that the spirit of Daniel Ninham and his braves protect the mountain.

There have been a number of reports of people who, while walking up the trail to the top of the summit, have heard Indian chanting and drums, but always in the distance. In 1996, Phil spoke at the local meeting of the New England Antiquities Research Association (NEARA) about the stone chambers and their connection to the ancient Celts. After the meeting he was approached by several people who told him a story about an encounter with an Indian phantom at Ninham Mountain several years ago. Below is the story as told to Phil.

The case involves several people who decided to hike up the trail to the top of the mountain on a brisk February day. As they approached the top of the mountain, out of nowhere appeared a tall man with long hair, wearing buckskins. His skin was dark. He was tall and wore deerskin

PLATE 1 Stone chamber in Putnam County, New York.

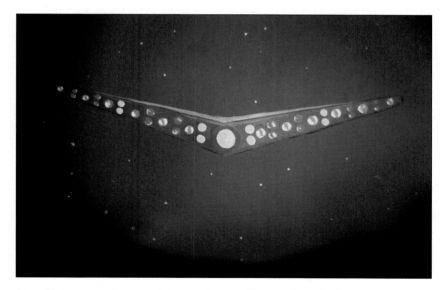

PLATE 2 Artist rendering of the Hudson Valley unidentified flying object.

PLATE 3 The Balanced Rock, Route 116, North Salem, New York.

PLATE 4 Washington Street chamber, New York.

PLATE 5 Gungywamp Equinox chamber; front view.

PLATE 6 Gungywamp Equinox chamber; Illuminaire shaft. The sun shines through here on the autumnal equinox.

PLATE 7 Fahnestock Park large chamber, showing standing stone (with numerous carvings) outside front entrance.

PLATE 8 Carved standing stone; Buddhist retreat, Temenos, Massachusetts.

PLATE 9 Oracle Chamber, America's Stonehenge, North Salem, New Hampshire.

PLATE 10 Sacrificial Table, America's Stonehenge, North Salem, New Hampshire.

PLATE 11 Summer Solstice Sunset Monolith, America's Stonehenge, North Salem, New Hampshire. The setting sun, on the first day of summer, lines up with this stone.

PLATE 12 Lion's Head, Kent Cliffs chamber, Kent Cliffs, New York.

PLATE 13 Chamber near Lion's Head, Kent Cliffs, New York. It's the site of much paranormal activity.

PLATE 14 Inside Route 301 chamber, Kent Cliffs, New York. The ghost of a Druid priest has been sighted here more than once.

PLATE 15 Stone chamber, Lockwood Lane, Putnam County, New York.

PLATE 16 Inside large solstice chamber, Whangtown Road, Kent Cliffs, New York. It is inside this chamber that Martin Brech had his experience (Chapter 10).

boots. His hair was tied in a ponytail, and his eyes were very dark. He approached the hikers and said hello. He then said that he just returned from the top of the mountain and would greatly appreciate it if they did not touch anything. When asked who he was the stranger simply replied, "I am the keeper of the mountain and servant of the spirits who live here." The man passed them and the hikers then walked for several seconds and turned around to get another look at him, but he was gone. According to the hikers there was no way that he could have moved out of their view since you can see up and down the trail for a considerable distance. They thought the entire incident was strange and proceeded to walk to the top of the mountain.

As they approached the top they noticed large amounts of snow which seemed to be piled over one particular location. It was as if it had just snowed over that area and they were amazed on how white it looked, like fresh snow, but there was not a cloud in the sky. As they walked over to the snow they noticed a crater in the center of the snow pile, around the crater was what they described as Indian signs of nature drawn into the snow. There was a turtle, bird, shooting star, and a figure of a warrior all carved deep in the snow and filled with a red substance which they thought was blood, but they weren't sure. They then began to get worried since they thought that some one was performing some type of ritual so they decided to leave the mountain. As they walked down the trail, to their right the strange Indian appeared again as if from nowhere. He walked across the path, stopped, and looked at them. He then said, "I am very sad that those who have followed me have not kept with the old ways. I have tried for many years to restore the power of this sacred place, but now I am tired and cannot continue for my power is also failing and the Great Spirit is asking me to move on." The man then started to walk to the left side of the trail and, according to the witnesses, simply vanished into thin air. The description of the man matches Daniel Ninham. Is his spirit still protecting the mountain? This is not the first case in which hikers and hunters have reported this apparition roaming the mountain.

A Journey into the Past

Ninham Mountain is saturated with energy. It is a place where gateways to another universe exist in our normal time and space. Since the area contains pockets of this energy then it may be possible that thoughts and impressions of the past might be locked in a kind of time loop. The theory states that the actions and thoughts of all living beings generate energy. Usually, this energy spreads out through the universe after the thought or action is completed, however sometimes the thought energy is contained in an energy field. If the theory is correct, then it might be possible for a sensitive person to tune in on these thought patterns from the past, and perhaps shed some light on some of the mysteries of Ninham Mountain.

In the past, our team worked with a number of psychics and had mixed results. We had to be sure that the information that we were getting was factual and could help with our research. Years ago Phil was introduced to Loretta Chaney, a woman who lives in Connecticut. Loretta is a gifted psychic who has worked with us on a number of investigations and has proven herself over and over again. Loretta's ability started at a very young age when she began to have out-of-body experiences. In her astral body, with the help of spirit guides, she was taken to other dimensions. To this day, Loretta has the ability to leave her body and consciously exists between two worlds. Loretta is not only a gifted psychic, but she also is involved with doing readings for people to help them communicate with their spirit guides. She also has developed an ability to take away pain, heal, and contact loved ones who have passed over to the other side.

Before Loretta was taken to Ninham Mountain, we took her to a number of stone chambers, and the Balanced Rock in North Salem, New York. Months before, with the assistance of Dr. Bruce Cornet, we were able to do extensive magnetic anomaly studies at several chamber locations. These studies along with graphs are presented in Appendix 2, page 135. Loretta was able find the center of the magnetic anomalies at each of these locations. She was so precise that at first it was very hard to believe—but then again, birds and certain animals are sensitive to changes in magnetic fields, so then why can't certain people? Scientifically it is possible, but it is a theory that has never been proven. This was enough proof to us that Loretta was indeed able to sense various types of energy fields. In the summer of 1997, we decided to take Loretta and her husband Scott to Ninham to see what she could tell us about this sacred place of the Wappinger tribe.

We arrived at Ninham Mountain on a very hot summer day, and proceeded to walk up the trail to the chamber and ritual area. Soon into our journey Loretta indicated that there was an Indian female spirit trying to make contact. She told Loretta that this was a sacred place, and once a long time ago her tribe lived peacefully before the white man came. She told Loretta that the bear was their animal spirit and her spirit is one of many who guard and protect the mountain. Without warning Loretta stopped and said that many spirits were trying to talk at once. Loretta then contacted her spirit guides to help filter out the communications and put some type of order in the contact so she would not be overwhelmed. This worked very well and she was able to continue and make sense out of what she was being told.

We moved up the trail, past the chamber to the ritual area, and sat on the quartz altar. Loretta said she saw men in Revolutionary war-era clothing, and that they were not supposed to be in that type of clothes. She said that there was a great sadness in the men and it seemed to be everywhere. She was perplexed as to what was being shown to her, since she saw many battles, fires, and military camps. We found this comment interesting since Daniel Ninham convinced his braves to fight for the English in the French and Indian War. His braves, who were forced to dress in English military uniforms, did not want to fight, but thought that the King of England would give back their land if they supported the English cause. Loretta was asked to go further back in time. She then reported that she saw large sheets of ice covering the area. Phil said, "Loretta, I asked you to go back, but not *that* far back, you're in the *Ice Age!*" She then placed her hands on some of the stones in the ritual area and kept on seeing Canada pop into her mind. We do know that most of the rocks in Putnam County were pushed down from Canada during the last Ice Age, which was 18,000 years ago.

Loretta's next impression was that she was being told that this was a location "where the earth breathes." She said that extraterrestrials are also attracted to this place for that reason. All of a sudden a rush of images and information came to Loretta, a rush so great she felt dizzy and had to sit down. She then saw Atlantians working side by side with the Indians a very long time ago. She told us that the Atlantians were a hybrid race, part human and part extraterrestrial, and they had a more advanced civilization than the rest of the world. She saw that the spots that now have chambers on them once had small pyramids. As Loretta moved forward in time she then saw ancient Phoenicians in the area and she claims that they were the ones who built the first chambers. After the pyramids weathered away the Indians marked the sacred ground with standing stones. The Phoenician traders and explorers built stone temples over these high energy areas and the later chambers were then built by the Celts with strong Druid influence.

Loretta began to get tired, so we started to walk down the road to return to the car. She said that something or someone was attempting to block her communications. She said that it was an old adversary of Phil's, an evil dark master of the black arts. The dark master wanted to make a deal for information about the chambers. Loretta called upon her spirit guides to block him out, and communications ceased at that point. We began to ask Loretta questions because it was clear that she received much more information that she talked about when we were still walking to the car. As we relaxed for a while we asked her if there was any possible way to use the chambers to generate some type of phenomena, so that it could be documented.

Portals to Another Reality

Loretta said that the chambers were portals to the other side used for traveling out-of-body. "First," she said, "in order for them to be activated, you have to condition your body and mind by meditating and fasting, but most importantly you must let go of this material world. The real difficult thing would be trying to find the right frequency of energy pulse to open the portal."

This seemed to make sense because the Druids believed that there are certain locations that they called holy ground, which at times open up a window or doorway to another universe. They believed that intelligent beings and other creatures came into our world at this time and it was possible for a human being to enter their world, although they considered this very dangerous. Loretta then said that the portals were not attached to any fixed location at the other side. If one passes through, then you may not be able to find your way back, you could wander through an infinite number of parallel realities.

Loretta's spirit guides also told her that a very long time ago the earth's energy field in these locations was much stronger since all the chambers were aligned through magnetic lines of force. This allowed the "spirits" from the other side to move freely through the portals and communicate with human beings. In recent times the chambers have gotten out of alignment because of modern-day construction and the destruction of a great number of them, and this has weakened their power considerably. As Loretta was talking she stopped and concentrated as if something was being told to her. She then said, "The chambers are portals to make passage to the other side easier without interference. People often came back to these locations to talk with loved ones who have passed over. This is the reason why these areas were looked at as sacred."

We then asked if it was possible to open up the portal and make the journey ourselves. She then said, "We don't have the understanding, technology, or frame of mind to produce the particular frequency needed to open the portal, but if we wanted to try the best time would be during the Spring Equinox." She concluded that one of the reasons the chambers are not working like they should is because of alien interference. According to what Loretta was told, the aliens have put a sort of lock on them so that they could only use the portal to travel from their world to ours. They are also partially responsible for the alignment problem since they sort of re-tuned some of the portals so they open up in their universe, and not the spirit world of the Druids.

With that the session ended. Although we felt we had more data to work with, the experience just created an entire new host of questions; questions we felt had to be answered for us to solve the mystery of Ninham Mountain.

CHAPTER 7

Journey into the Unknown

$\mathbf{W}$E WERE NOW CONVINCED that the chambers in the Hudson Valley were built by at least three different cultures. The first were Phoenician traders and explorers who sailed across the Atlantic Ocean around 2500 B.C. They may have also been joined by Greek sailors looking for tin and copper to make bronze. These two cultures may have continued their journey into the New World until about 45 B.C. Apparently they kept the existence of the new land a secret from the rest of the world because they found a country that was rich in natural resources. The second culture to land in the northeastern United States were the ancient Celts.

The Celts were primarily explorers and, unlike the Greeks and Phoenicians who were looking for valuable ores, the Celts were most interested in the animal life since there is a great deal of evidence that they hunted, then shipped back to Europe furs and fine leathers. The last group of ancient visitors to North America were the early Irish-Celtic Christians. Our research indicates that they built the chambers not only in northern Connecticut, but also in New Hampshire, Massachusetts, and Vermont.

The first Irish Christian explorers landed in New England sometime between A.D. 400–500 and they continued to make the trip across the ocean until about A.D. 1300. We are quite sure that St. Brendan the Navigator was not the first to make the journey from his time period, but he definitely was one of the first Irish monks to do so. We now had to find more evidence and began to look very closely at each site. Since the chambers were built such a long time ago, much of the evidence was lost, so we had to journey backward in time and imagine what New England was like countless centuries ago.

The Stone Cutters

In some of the chambers we found drill marks in the stone showing how it was cut from the nearby bedrock (see Figure 7.1, below). These drill marks were identical at all sites, indicating that the same technique was used to cut the stone. The drill used to cut the rock seemed to be operated by hand with perhaps abrasive-like sand to help wear away

FIGURE 7.1 Drill marks in stone at chamber site.

the stone. The drill marks that we found could not be matched with known ones that were used in the eighteenth and nineteenth centuries. Some of the chambers do not contain stones with drill marks, and it could be that these chambers were built by a culture who did not drill the stone. They may have used blocks of stone and shaped them so that they could fit into place in the walls or ceilings of the chambers.

One other method that could have been used to cut the stone was a simple procedure that was used by cultures in the northern latitudes. Sections of rock were found that had cracks in them, then in the winter water was poured into the cracks causing it to freeze. As the water becomes ice it contracts, then expands, causing the rock to split. We have found multiple cases where this technique was used to take the rock from the bedrock. The rock was then rubbed against a harder rock using sand as an abrasive until it became smooth and would fit into a particular section of wall.

For minerals that were very hard another technique may have been used to cut them. We know that crystals have a definite geometric atomic structure. Although crystals are very hard, most of them are brittle and will break evenly if hit in the right location. For example, a diamond cutter knows exactly where to strike the diamond getting it to break at certain desired angles. If he is off a micrometer, the gem cracks the wrong way and becomes flawed and worthless. It seems that whoever cut the quartz at Ninham Mountain knew exactly how to strike the mineral at a particular angle with the proper amount of force, creating a clean break. For one to be able to do this they would have to have knowledge of the molecular structure of the crystal lattice in the mineral. Today the geological term is called *fracture*.

We decided we would call in an expert with great experience working with stones. Marianne's father, Jack Allen, had many years of knowledge as a mine owner in Idaho Springs, Colorado. He did us the favor of taking a close look at the work that we were doing and what follows is a transcript of his notes.

Marianne and Phil took me on a tour to see some things nearby in New York. They have been studying what appear to me to be neolithic chambers and the chambers do appear to be quite old. I have seen old workings in England and I have visited many American Indian "places" in the United States. This has included many Southwestern Pueblos, Cliff Dwellings, and similar constructions. This has also included the structures in Canyon DeChelly in Arizona and Chaco Canyon in New Mexico.

In England I got to see Stonehenge, Woodhenge, the Avebury Rings, and most of the nearby ancient monuments. That did include the Long Barrow Chamber near the Avebury Rings, which was similar to the chambers that I saw in New York. Objects that have been around for only 100 years and even up to 200 years do not have the patina of "age" that older structures get. The structures that have been around, out in the weather and wind, for extended periods, such as 600 years, do get a weather-beaten look that is hard to miss and probably almost as hard to fake. So the chambers that I saw in New York have a look that says to me that they are quite old for man-made structures.

I was told that these chambers were storage cellars for early colonists from Europe. I think it is more than a little unlikely. The colonists were never famous for their rock work and never did much with the rocks that were around except to remove many that were in fields that they wanted to till. No, I have to believe that if colonists had built these chambers, the stories we have been handed down would include many more chapters on the work that went into the building of them. There is much work and effort in each one of these chambers and there are many of them in New England. In addition, there are long walls that seem to be associated with the chambers and even these walls represent a considerable effort.

The walls are seldom as much as three feet high, made of numerous small and medium rocks. Yet even this gathering of rocks was done with considerable care and even though we do not know to what end they were built for, they have an obvious placement and direction. Considering the length of some of these walls, they are of surprisingly uniform cross section. Since they appear to be made of local rocks, they can not be absolutely uniform in cross section, yet the work is rather impressive. Walls may go for several hundred yards. There are bends and curves, again to no known purpose at the present, but the placement looks as if it might have been very purposeful at the time the wall was put in.

The rock work in the chambers appears to be of a challenging nature. The chambers were about six feet high inside, by ten to fifteen feet deep and around six to seven feet wide. That does not seem too large, except that the ceiling is covered by three, four, or five large rocks put up there crossways. That makes these rocks at least seven feet long, and from one to two feet wide. They just have to be a foot or two thick, or they would collapse under their own weight and the weight of a minimum of a foot of dirt and rocks placed on top of each chamber. That makes each ceiling rock in the range of from 0.1 to 1.3 cubic yards. That means they can easily weigh from 500 pounds to close to three tons. That is not the kind of thing that you trivially move around.

Water weighs just over 62 pounds per cubic foot. So a cubic yard of water would weigh perhaps 1,674 pounds. Typical rock has a density of around 2.5, though many rocks can be quite different than that. So, for the typical rock, its weight for a cubic yard might me in the range of 4185 pounds. For the sake of ease and simplicity, take the conversion number as two tons per yard and keep in mind that many rocks will vary significantly.

There are a couple of other little details of interest in these chambers. The first is that the ceilings do not leak. The side walls do slant inward in some chambers, and it looks as if the walls would collapse if the ceiling rocks were removed. In some chambers, the side walls are almost vertical and the walls might hold themselves. There is an interesting question of how the slant-walled chambers were built.

I conjecture that because the walls slant inward toward the top of the chamber, they might have been built with dirt holding up the walls until the top was in position. Then, with the top firmly in position, the dirt could be removed and you would have an impressively slanted set of side walls. It would not have had to have been done in that way, but as long as it could have been done, it is not impossible and the fact that the feat was done is quite impressive.

I did not get to see the floor in any of the chambers that I visited. I have to believe that even the floor would be of considerable interest. It, too, is made of carefully fitted rocks? How deep do they go? Are they the same kind of rocks that make up the sides and roof? Are there any fossils or pollen grains down there to indicate anything more about the age of the chambers? Is there any wood or charcoal to help with dating of the active times of the chamber? Any of the questions that normally would be answered, might be assisted by studies of the floors of these chambers. My impression is that the floor of many caves in Europe has netted much information about the history of the caves and the users.

In some chambers there are rocks that have what look like modern drill holes. I got to see one up close and my impression is that it was done with a stick (or several). If you take some straight sticks, a bow drill or some equivalent, water, and sand, with lots of time and patience, you can drill long, straight, and nearly constant diameter holes. With enough patience, you can make holes up to several feet in length. These holes when filled with water in the winter, will hold the water until the cold temperatures cause the water to freeze. When the water freezes and expands, if there are sufficient number of holes, the rock will crack. This is an excellent way to shape what is otherwise a very hard rock. I found a drill hole in a chamber entrance portal rock. I estimated the rock weighs upwards of 750 pounds. If it was cut off of a larger rock, special for the entranceway, then it makes the chamber even more interesting. I have worked in a mine in the Idaho Springs area in Colorado and I am more than a little experienced with large rocks. They are uniformly heavy and hard to work with. I have also lost a couple of friends that accidentally found themselves trying to hold up one and two yards of rocks that have fallen from the roof of their mine tunnels.

Lost Secrets

In our modern society, we have a multitude of tools that have helped us build our great cities, but 3,000 years ago this was not the case. So how were great structures like these chambers built? No one seems to know for sure, but it seems that our ancestors had some type of knowledge of not only how to cut the stone, but also to move massive slabs of rock great heights. We still don't know exactly how the great pyramids of Egypt were built, and we still gaze in wonder when we look at the stonework of the churches in Europe built by the Freemasons. The Freemason Society was a organization of masons that formed in the Middle Ages, who were the keepers of hidden knowledge. In order to keep their independence in a time of corrupt kings, they kept this information very secret. It was said that the Freemasons knew the ancient ways on how to work the stone, secrets that were handed down to them from the time of the pyramids. Legend says that the leaders of the Freemasons had a secret power that was able to make large stones much lighter so that they can be lifted to great heights with little trouble. This is supposedly how they moved the large stones to the top of the churches in the Middle Ages. To keep the technique hidden, they only worked at night, under the cover of darkness. Was the same procedure used to build the chambers?

We started to wonder and began to do some research into the Freemason Society. Even though the organization still exists today, it has become somewhat of a service club for businessmen, and the ancient mysticism of long ago that motivated them is now lost in the past. No Freemason that we talked to had any idea about the stonework that founders of the society did long ago. Like the chambers, the knowledge was lost to the past.

The Spirit of the Lion

To many cultures the lion represents royalty, strength, and courage. At one time lions, like bears, were common around the world. In New England, mountain lions were one of the primary predators in the food chain and since they were such a threat to livestock, they were all killed out before the turn of the nineteenth century. However, lions were long extinct in Europe during the time of the Celts and were not found in the British Islands. The lion is a fierce predator and a very powerful force of nature. The Celts believed that by harnessing an animal's spirit you could obtain that animal's power and become "one with it." This belief was later similar to the Native American ritual of a person finding their animal spirit and merging with it during times of trouble to obtain its wisdom and power.

When the ancient Celts came to New England they encountered mountain lions and were no doubt impressed by the strength and courage of the beast, so they carved rocks and stones in their likeness to capture the animal's power. The Balanced Rock in North Salem, New York, is a carved rock. One side looks like a long-nosed animal, perhaps a lion, and the other side looks like a short-nosed animal, perhaps a cougar or some other close relative of the lion. The Balanced Rock itself generates a great deal of energy in the form of an intense negative magnetic anomaly. This has been measured and the results of this study can be found in Appendix 2 (see page 135). However, there may be another form of energy that is being channeled through the massive stone and that is the spiritual energy of nature. It is this energy that makes one feel elated or strong when one drops one's conscious mind and allows the Balanced Rock's energy to flow through one.

Recently, a group of people who belong to a psychic guild visited the rock and made a circle around it. As they began to focus their minds and allowed the energy to encircle them, they all seemed to lose touch with this world. They all began to chant, and at that point one could feel the energy that was being directed through them from the rock. The entire area seemed charged up as the group continued for several minutes. After they finished there was no doubt that they had accomplished something, since everyone present felt energetic and refreshed.

We also know that many great warriors throughout time symbolized themselves with a powerful beast; one such example was Richard, the Lion Hearted. It is possible that some great Celtic warrior was buried under the Balanced Rock, which could have been used as a marker for his grave. The stone may have been shaped with a double lion head as a testimony to this person's strength and mettle as a warrior. There were also some cultures that had powerful animals as the symbol of their country. The ancient city of Babylon was identified as a fierce lion on the attack. Although this may sound strange to some, we should remind you that the symbol for the United States is a powerful bird of prey, the bald eagle.

In the town of Kent Cliffs, New York, there is a well-preserved oval chamber that has a very old wall in the front of it. On the wall is the carved head of a lion. The head of the lion is surrounded by a number of rocks that have been shaped at angles, outlining the head and providing a frame for it. The chamber itself is one of the best in Putnam County, and inside it are rocks that are carved in the shape of a bison, tortoise, and a half moon. Once again, the builders may have been trying to capture the power of the animal's spirit to enhance the chamber's energy. It was in this chamber that some people have reported the appearance of strange lights and flashes of energy. Recently, we found one other location that has a carved rock in the shape of a lion. Since it is on private property we cannot give its exact location but can say it is in northern Putnam County, New York, in the town of Fishkill. There are several rocks all in a circle, and the rock to the south is shaped in the form of a long-nosed lion. The eyes of the lion are closed and face to the west. The Celts believed that when the soul left this earth it traveled on a westerly course to follow the setting sun. This could be one of the reasons why many of the chambers point to the east (birth), and to the west (death).

Digging into the Past

"The chambers are sterile from an archeological point of view." Those words were repeated to us over and over again by archaeologists. In order to prove to the world of academia that the chambers are very old we had to find some type of artifact that could tie together their construction to a specified time period.

After digging in several chambers, we found nothing. We even brought in a metal detector with the hope of finding bronze—that would help prove our theory; however we found nothing that would convince the skeptics. As we dug in several chambers, we encountered a complex network of underground roots. The soil was twelve inches deep in most places, and because of the roots it was almost impossible to go down any further. Digging up a small section in one chamber required an entire day and the use of numerous tools. We did a test pit in three chambers, and in each one we found that after digging from eight to twelve inches, we hit slabs of rock. This was not the bedrock, but large flat rocks that seemed to make up the floor. Phil commented that he thought it unusual that someone would go to so much trouble to build such a sturdy magnificent stone structure then settle for a dirt floor. This was not the case, it was apparent that the chambers (at least the ones we dug in) had a stone floor and the dirt settled there over a very long period of time. This provided further evidence that the chambers were constructed a very long time ago and not during the eighteenth century. But, how long ago?

It is possible to determine how long it would take for the soil to accumulate to that depth. Of course, this is not an absolute way of dating the age of the chambers, but we could get an approximate age. The calculations showed us that the chambers we investigated were a minimum of 2,000 years old, which would place their construction somewhere around 5 B.C. In one site we lifted up the rock and discovered an entirely new soil horizon. We then dug to a depth of six inches and came to a thick yellow clay. We had now gone back to a time just after the last Ice Age, which is about 18,000 years ago. This showed us that our initial figures may have been wrong since this indicated that the chambers may be as old as 5,000 years and constructed around 3000 B.C. We left more confused than ever, but this study did show that modern archaeology was very wrong about the time period of construction. The stone chambers could be much older than even we thought.

The Fires of Yesterday

In spite of all the evidence that pointed out the chambers were very old, we still had the burden of proof trying to place them within a particular time period. Scientists demand hard evidence, and it was apparent that the only way we were going to get the skeptics to listen to us was to find some type of an artifact. In 1992, we showed a number of people the two chambers in Fahnestock Park, New York. We had plenty of help that day, and our main focus was to look more closely in the walls and some of the secret pockets that exist between the ceiling and the floor. The smaller chamber was nicknamed by us "the tomb," because it went slightly underground and in the back was a slab that was cut out of the bedrock and shaped to hold a human body.

In this chamber we did some digging along the bottom part of the walls and discovered a small area that was no more than two by three feet. We found a number of pieces of anthracite (hard coal). Anthracite was used long ago as a fuel source for fires. Since this type of coal is much denser than normal coal (bituminous) it burns longer and hotter. Anthracite is not found in the area and it must have been brought in and placed in the storage area of the chamber shortly after it was built. The coal could have been brought in by the Celts, or whoever built this chamber to use as a heat source in the winter time. The hard coal did pique the interest of the Archaeology Department at Central Connecticut State University, since it was a natural coal and typical of a fuel used by ancient people rather than the factory-processed coal we use today for barbecues.

Unknown Remains

We then proceeded to the second chamber, only about 200 yards from the first. This chamber is one of the largest in Putnam County, and because of this we call it the "King's Chamber." We began to dig, and found the remains of calcified bones that looked like they belonged to some type of bird. We also found several strange bones that did not resemble any type of animal common to the area; they looked like human bones. The bones were only fragments, but they looked like part of a human finger, but we could not say for sure.

Later we brought the bones to a medical expert who stated that it was almost impossible to tell what they were, but they looked like the index finger of a man. We were also told that the bones were "calcified," which is a state where the moisture has been extracted, and the mineral remains harden and become resistant to decay. Calcification is one of the steps before a bone becomes fossilized. If the people who built the chambers did bury their dead or what remained after they burned the bodies, it is highly unlikely that any one will find the entire skeletal remains of an ancient Celt. This is because the acidity in the soil is so high that the bones would dissolve within 300 years, which is very quick when compared to geologic time. The soil in that area is so acidic that farmers have to mix lime (calcium carbonate) in the soil to neutralize the acidity so that plants can grow.

The Dagger

As we examined the inside of the King's Chamber more closely, Phil warned the rest of our party not to stick their hands between the cracks of the rocks because of spiders. Although the spider is a shy creature, it may bite and some of the spiders in the area are poisonous. Nevertheless, one young man with us stuck his hand in a long space in the wall. "Indy," he jokingly called out to Phil. "I think I found something." He then pulled out a black knife-like object that looked like a spearhead. The artifact was perfectly preserved and was eight inches long (Figure 7.2, below). It was made of obsidian (volcanic glass), and was sharp enough to stick in wood and cut paper. This was some type of ceremonial knife since it looked much too perfect to have been used as weapon or tool. Obsidian is not found in the area, so somebody must have brought it in from somewhere else and placed it in the chamber. From its location in the chamber it looked like it was in there a very

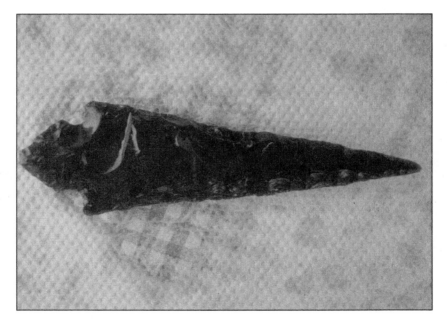

FIGURE 7.2 Obsidian dagger found in large chamber, Fahnestock Park, New York.

long time and somebody did a good job concealing it. It also appeared as if the space in the wall was built to hold the knife and keep it secure.

Phil then wanted the opinion of a skeptical archaeologist, so he picked a person who has been critical of Phil's work involving the chambers in the past. This particular archaeologist had just returned from a dig and was in his lab sifting through tiny pieces of flint and Indian "scrapers" when Phil arrived. He told Phil, "I just got back from this dig and we discovered a prehistoric site in Connecticut that was Indian." Phil said, "Are you sure it was Indian?" The archaeologist replied, "What else could it be?" Phil did not want to get in a heated discussion about the possibility that it may not be American Indian, but Celtic, so he began to examine the finds. The archaeologist seemed quite proud and excited over the tiny bits of shell and bone that he found. Phil then pulled out the obsidian dagger and said, "Well, what do you think of this?" The archaeologist's mouth dropped open. He said, "Where did you get that?" Phil told him how it was found in the King's Chamber. The archaeologist then responded, "Why don't you let me take it and have the people at Norwalk and Connecticut State look at it, and I'll give it back in a few days?" Phil quickly said no. The archaeologist then said, "Phil, I really don't want to tell you about the law in this matter. The law states that no artifact found is to be removed from an archeological site, unless a certified archaeologist is present." Phil then replied quickly, "Well, I guess the law does not apply to this since you've been telling me for years that these are not archeological sites." Phil then decided that the analysis of the dagger should be carried out by an outsider, someone who has no connection with the area and is open-minded about the origin of the stone chambers.

The dagger was taken to archaeologists at the University of Pennsylvania, where it underwent a variety of tests. The shape and design of the dagger, when compared with other artifacts, showed that no similar objects had ever been found in North America. This means that the dagger was brought in from somewhere else. The second test was an analysis of the obsidian. Since obsidian, which is often referred to as volcanic glass, is an intrusive igneous rock (a rock formed under the surface of the earth by the cooling and solidification of magma), it would be possible to determine where it came from by its chemical makeup. The initial tests showed that the obsidian used to make the dagger came from Iceland or perhaps Greenland. The only way that the object could be dated, other than comparing it with similar artifacts is something called a "moisture absorption test rate." Obsidian absorbs water vapor at a steady rate as soon as its exposed to the air. Although this does not tell us the exact age of the dagger it does give us an approximate time when it was cut and shaped.

The preliminary analysis of the test showed it to be at least 4,000 years old, which would place it around 2000 B.C. This does not mean that the chamber was built at that time, it means that the dagger was placed in this chamber a very long time ago and was brought in from northern Europe or perhaps Greenland. It is possible that the ancient Celts had the dagger in their possession for a long time and brought it over when they started to explore the east coast of North America during the end of the Bronze Age.

The dagger is the first real artifact found and its discovery has caused a sensation in the world of archaeology. The die-hard skeptics, however, consider it an impossible find and have even accused Phil of planting it in the chamber, but where would he even get such an ancient tool especially when its value as a museum piece has been estimated at over $5,000? We won the battle for credibility, but the war was far from over.

CHAPTER 8

Doorways to Another Dimension

MOST PEOPLE THINK OF space as "emptiness," but space is a fabric that can be bent, twisted, and turned inside out. Matter has the ability to warp (or curve) space around it, thus the sun (which makes up 99.99 percent of all the mass in the solar system) warps large volumes of space. The warping of space is what gravity is all about. According to present theory, there is enough matter in the visible universe to make space warp around it, thus closing it. This means that we exist in a very large bubble universe.

If you leave in a spaceship traveling at the speed of light and travel in what you think is a straight line, you will eventually (about 20 billion years later) end up at the point at which you started. Light even follows the curvature of space. This was proven in the early twentieth century by Albert Einstein and his unified theory of relativity. Stranger still, the more you warp space, the slower time runs. The theory simply says that time is relative to the observer and the more intense the gravitational field, the greater the curvature of space and the slower your time will run. This means that time on planet Earth is running a tiny bit slower than time on the moon.

Decades after Einstein's death, scientists finally developed the technology to test the theory. In 1986, two radioactive clocks were calibrated to read the same time. A radioactive clock measures the decay of the atomic nucleus and can divide a second into 100 billion parts. One of these clocks was left on the surface of Earth while the other was taken in a high-altitude jet plane. In theory, the gravity pulling on the jet plane is less since it is further from the center of Earth, so according to theory its time should run faster. After several hours of flight the jet finally landed and the clocks were compared. The scientists who conducted the experiment were delighted, but not surprised to find that the clock on Earth to be 10 billionths of a second slower than the airborne clock. Although this may not sound like much, it does prove the time-dilation theory. This opens up the possibilities of time travel, which before was only the subject of science fiction. What does all this mean? According to this theory, at the formation of the universe, an infinite number of bubble universes with multiple dimensions were formed, interlacing each other in a four-dimensional manner.

When Time Began

When the universe was formed, there was a great explosion of energy. Matter did not exist at this time. As the energy expanded, it cooled down to form the first particles, then the particles formed a simple element, hydrogen. The massive clouds of hydrogen formed the first galaxies and stars, and the universe continued to expand. Much of the matter formed together in large clumps warping space around them creating a vast number of bubble universes.

You can visualize this effect if you take a tube and blow air into a bowl of soapy water. The bubbles that form interlace with each other in a three-dimensional fashion. Although this is a simple example, it can give you an idea of what took place. Pockets of matter trapped in their bubble universes continued to evolve and a first generation of stars created all the heavy elements in their massive cores by nuclear fusion. These stars burned very hot and soon ended their life by blowing to bits and seeding each universe with all the elements heavier than hydrogen. The heavy elements formed a new generation of stars (such as our sun) and planets. Everything that we have on this Earth today, even the material that makes up our bodies, was fused in a stellar core countless billions of years ago.

Time is merely an illusion; humans use it to measure motion. Our own time on this planet is based on Earth's rotation and revolution. The space between the bubble universes exist in a four-dimensional state where time does not exist. Here the past, present, and future all coexist together. Scientists have found that as your mass increases—or the closer you get to the velocity of light—the slower your time runs. Why is this? The answer is a little complex, but we will try to make it as simple as possible without getting into quantum physics. Planet Earth is a sphere with a certain amount of gravity. If you take off in a jet from New York and continue toward the east you will observe that the jet is traveling in a straight line. This is not the case—the jet is, in fact, moving in an arc and following the curvature of the Earth. If the jet continues on its course, it will arrive once again at New York, but it will be approaching from the west. If the jet should exceed the escape velocity of Earth, which is about seven miles a second, then it will no longer follow Earth's curvature, and will shoot out into space.

Traveling through the universe we experience the same thing. If we travel at the speed of light (in the our spaceship of the imagination), we might think we are moving in a straight line, but in reality we are following the curvature of space. If we exceed the speed of light, we no longer follow this curve and shoot off into another nearby universe. As we approach the vast space between the universes, time slows down to zero, since here there is no time, and all points of existence exist together. It is possible that we don't have to reach the speed of light to escape our bubble universe. If space can be warped by an electromagnetic pulse, it could create a sort of wormhole (or tunnel) to the fourth dimension. The chambers in New England may, in fact, be the "energy generators" that accomplish this, making interdimensional travel possible.

Passage of the Spirit

As stated earlier, there is evidence that some of the gallery chambers may have been used to hold a human body until it was properly prepared by a Druid priest. This is what the chamber and the ritual area on Ninham Mountain was used for. The Druids believed that when a person died, his spirit had to be contained until it was conditioned to pass to the other world. The body was placed in the chamber and somehow the priest activated an energy field that enclosed the chamber, holding the spirit until it was ready to pass on. They believed that when the body died, the spirit would travel to different levels on the other side. The level in which the spirit went depended upon who you were in this life and what you accomplished. The priest would open the correct passage way so the soul of that person could travel and be placed in the correct location in the spirit world. When the proper door was opened, the energy field was released and the spirit could leave and continue its destiny on the other side. It may be possible that several of these spirits never made it to the other side and are still trapped inside the chambers.

We have a number of reports where people have seen what appears to be an ancient Celt or a Druid priest materialize in a chamber. There are also other cases where psychics, who have visited the chambers, claim that the spirit of one of the builders tried to contact them. This passage to the other world may have worked two ways. The souls of earthly beings were allowed to travel through the doorways, but powerful spirits were also allowed to enter our universe from the other side. This ritual was very important to the ancient Celts, because many of these spirits came over to our side as teachers of knowledge.

The Ritual of Stone

The ritual to invoke these spirits was simple. Standing stones were placed in the earth in a circle. The stones were carved in a conical shape and contained a great deal of fine crystal. The distance between each stone was important; the number of the stones was usually twelve with a thirteenth stone placed in the center. The stone in the center was held by a Druid priest and was much smaller than the others, and more rounded. At certain times of the year, the priest and twelve others would form a circle around the stones, with the priest in the center. The rest of the procedure is unknown, but something was done to allow energy to be channeled from the Earth through each of the stones in the circle.

When this was accomplished, the stones began to glow and a band of energy would jump from stone to stone and then the energy would be focused to the inner circle, to the stone being held by the priest. At this point a portal would open up, and spirits from the other side would come into our world. These "spirits" looked like spheres of light of various colors and would dance around the area inside the circle for a certain length of time. Then they would fly into the stone held by the priest, the priest would fall to the ground. Hours later he would awaken with great knowledge of the sciences and of the future.

Return of the Old Gods

In Ireland the appearance of strange lights is a common sight. There are many stories of globes of lights seen around the old Druid ritual grounds—they are what remains of the old gods after the saints of the Christians stripped them of their power. They were once powerful gods and now, according to local mythology, have been reduced to fairies and spirits of Earth. In County Kerry, Ireland, these lights are seen just about every night in and around a location that was once a very important ritual area for the Druids. This location has many standing stones arranged in a circle. The stones are conical in shape, and form a circle with a thirty-five foot diameter.

A light the size of a basketball has been seen bouncing off each stone, and then moving away and floating silently less than five feet above the ground. The light is yellow in color, but there have been reports of it changing color from blue to red as it hovered. When people approach the light, it moves away, but according to reports, they say that if you stay still, then it will slowly approach you. The light behaves like there is an intelligence behind it, but this intelligence acts more like an animal than an sentient being. Is this strange light one of the "spirits" that was brought through the doorway and became trapped in our world?

Such light phenomena has been known as "spook lights" and has been reported all over the world. The following examples of this spook light phenomena in the United States are the Marfa, Texas lights, and the ghost lights on Reservoir Road in the town of Southeast, New York. We personally investigated the Southeast report since it took place within a one half-hour drive from our home.

The Marfa Lights of Texas

The most famous of the American spook lights can be found in the state of Texas in the small town of Marfa, 300 kilometers southeast of El Paso. Although the lights do not appear every night, they are said to be quite regular, and even visitors to the area have claimed to have seen them. The first recorded incidence took place in 1883, where cattleman thought they were Apache campfires, but soon realized that they were something strange. The lights were seen floating up and down and moving back and forth. The lights have been reported as having a yellow color and sometimes have been noticed to flicker. Several of them have been seen frolicking around, even chasing each other like small baby animals at play.

In 1973, a team of geologists who heard about the lights went to Marfa to carry out observations between March and June. During one outing in March they did see the lights, but as they tried to get closer, the lights moved away and kept their distance from them. On March 20, the scientists observed the lights for twenty minutes. They began swinging in the air, rocking back and forth then started looping around each other. One of the geologists commented that they appeared to be playing. Since 1986, the lights have been seen quite often and photographed many times. The lights were known by the Apache of that region for over 100 years and were perceived as spirits. According to settlers during the late nineteenth century, the lights were ghosts of massacred Indians. Later on, in the early twentieth century, Texans believed that the lights were spirits that guarded hidden treasures.

Whatever the Marfa lights really are, they have a striking resemblance to similar phenomenon reported on ancient Druid sacred ground in the British Isles. A similar example of this phenomenon can be found in Hudson Valley, New York, in the small, old mining town of Southeast. The spook light that has been reported here is almost identical to the Marfa and the Druid lights. Legend says that the light represents the ghosts of three miners who were killed in a nearby cave-in of the Tilly Foster Mine in 1885. It is said that the spirits of the three miners wander up and down the road trying to let people know who they were in life, since there were no records kept of the names of the workers.

The Spook Light of Southeast, New York

During summer, 1993, an associate of Phil's, a physicist in New Jersey, proposed a theory. He suggested that phenomena like the "ghost lights" of Reservoir Road are rarely seen or not seen at all, because at times they are invisible to the naked eye. He felt that if blue sensitive film was used in conjunction with a dark blue filter, the phantom lights may show in a photograph. Phil's assistance was requested. However, hanging out until all hours of the summer night on some lonely dark road didn't seem appealing to him since the odds of seeing something were astronomical. He declined. Nevertheless, the physicist set up a camera on a tripod with special film ready to shoot anything that looked remotely strange. Below is a transcript of what took place that night as told to us several days after his encounter.

I got to the location at 10:00 P.M. on May 21, 1994. I drove around for a while and finally decided to park on the far end of lower Magnetic Mine Road, which for some reason is marked as part of Reservoir Road on the map. I set up the camera, loaded with the special blue light-sensitive film, and waited.

About an hour passed I then began to feel uneasy, like I was being watched. I thought it was nothing since I was on this lonely dark road where people have reported UFOs, alien creatures, and ghosts. I then looked down the dirt road and saw what looked like a fog. The fog then formed a sphere that was, I would say, about two feet in diameter.

As I watched, it began to pulsate. I then shot a number of frames. I got curious and started to approach the cloud.

As I got closer to the cloud, it slowly moved away, keeping its distance from me. I went back to the camera and the ball of fog started to approach me. It was about 150 feet away and then it moved up and down covering a span of about five feet or less. As I watched, it started vibrating and began to change color. The change was barely noticeable and I was hoping that I got something on film. This went on for about ten minutes, then the light just vanished. When I had the film developed I was surprised to see the images came out so bright. I guess I was right when I suspected that the phenomena radiates at the violet end of the spectrum.

Needless to say we were impressed with the photographs that he took. They showed a brilliant light ionizing the area around it and rapidly changing frequency in the blue-violet area of the spectrum. It seems that the phenomenon shifted so far into the ultraviolet that it became invisible to the eye and finally to even the special film he was using. It is strange to think that this "spook light" may be all around us and we just don't see it because our eyes are not sensitive to that area of the electromagnetic spectrum.

Frozen in Time

As mentioned earlier in chapter 3 there is an area in the Gungywamp complex called the Cliff of Tears. This location sits on top of a massive deposit of pure iron ore in the form of magnetite. According to David Barron, who is in charge of the Gungywamp site, the Cliff of Tears got its name several years ago when he lead a group of people on a tour of the area. David told us: "We had just finished most of the tour and had arrived at the Cliff of Tears when an elderly woman stepped forward and had large tears flowing down her cheeks. She gave me a smile and apologetically said, 'I don't know why I am crying, I actually feel quite happy, but here they are!' I replied, 'Don't be concerned. You are about the eighteenth person to have this happen. We don't understand the cause, but there have been folks who also experienced nosebleeds, sudden onset of menstruation, bleeding gums, and most of all, tears.' She was immediately relieved and said to one and all 'Well, this must be the Cliff of Tears.' The name stuck and since that time we have discovered that a huge vein of magnetite, reversed in polarity, extends through the cliff. This has a significant effect on lowering blood pressure, causing a flow toward the extremities, fine capillaries, etc. I suspect this is one reason why birds avoid the area, since the lodestone confuses and disorients them."

It is said that people who visit the Cliff of Tears experience a variety of unusual paranormal phenomenon plus strange physiological effects. Some of these occurrences have already been presented earlier and now we will relate to you a story that was told to us by a scientific researcher, the late Charles Boyle, who had a great interest in the Gungywamp complex. The incident that follows was told to us a number of years ago, and we feel it is an important addition to our research since it is a case that involves time dilation.

I had been very interested in ancient civilizations and the possibility that the Gungywamp complex had been constructed by Bronze Age seafaring Europeans. So during the summer of 1991, I visited the complex with six other people hoping to find some documentation that would satisfy my curiosity.

After looking at the main complex and the chambers I noticed what I thought was etchings on a large rock near what is called the "Solstice Chamber." As I took a closer look I realized that they were not natural scratches in the rock, but it looked to me like an ancient form of Phoenician. I had always heard that many ancient people built sites such as this, over ground that contained a high content of energy. I was told about the Cliff of Tears and the incidents where people who walked into that area experienced bleeding from the eyes, ears, and sometimes the nose. I had also heard stories about physiological effects, that is changes in their vital signs, which include pulse and blood pressure. It could be that the energy in the area is focused at the Cliff of Tears, so I had to go there to find out for myself.

We all journeyed up the path that lead to the Cliff of Tears, as we entered I noticed a very large amount of iron ore that was scattered all over the place and some of it looked like it had fallen down the hill in some sort of avalanche. As we got closer to the actual cliff a few of the party members said that they felt dizzy, and I felt a little lightheaded myself. At that point I heard a sound that caught my attention and I looked away from the group. When I looked back, they all looked like statues, like they were frozen. This was really bizarre because there was no movement anywhere not even a sound from a bird, it was as if time stood still. This lasted about ten seconds, then, without warning, I once again heard sounds and the people I was with started moving and talking as if nothing happened. I ran over to them and asked them if they had noticed anything strange, but they looked at me as if I were strange. I told them what had just transpired, and they said according to their point of view nothing happened, everyone was moving normally. I know something very unusual took place; perhaps the energy in the area actually did something to the movement of time.

It is quite possible that the energy generated at the Cliff of Tears was strong enough to cause a "time dilation" effect. The only explanation for this would be if our normal space was brought closer to the fourth dimension. As mentioned earlier, four-dimensional space acts as a buffer between our world and a parallel reality. In this buffer there is no time, and as one moves closer to the four-dimensional state, someone viewing them from our normal reality may see them "frozen in time." Theoretically, once you cross the fourth dimension, you once again enter linear time in another universe. The evidence suggests that UFOs may be using the location of the chambers as sort of a doorway into their universe. The following case, related to us in 1987, is of a UFO encounter that took place very close to the chamber on Reservoir Road in Southeast, New York.

Taken into Another Dimension

The witnesses are two lawyers and their wives, all of whom were returning home from New York City after seeing a Broadway show. As they left the train station in their car, the driver decided to take a short cut through the Croton Falls–Southeast area, which is located on the border of Putnam and Westchester counties. They turned down a very dark desolate road called Reservoir Road, which is about two miles long with no streetlighting. Normally the driver would never take this road, but on this night he felt almost compelled to do so. He later told us, "It was as if I was almost programmed to take the road, I could not steer around it, I didn't want to take it, because I have a new car and I knew it was unpaved with many holes, but I drove down it any way."

As they proceeded down Reservoir Road, the car's engine began to sputter, and then went dead. Although the lights on the car still worked, the engine would not turn over. The two men sat in the front seat, and their wives were in the back. They all decided that they would wait for a car to pass or one of the men would try to walk to a nearby home and make a phone call for help. It was late July, and the night was very warm, so they rolled down the windows to get some air. The driver's friend (the other lawyer) heard something moving in the wooded area off to the right. He grabbed a flashlight in the glove compartment and got out of the car to the side of the road. As he shined his light in the woods, the others called out to him, "What do you see, what's making all that noise?" The man stood there motionless and made no sound, then without warning he ran back into the car, slammed the door and rolled up the window and yelled, "Let's get out of here! I think they're from outer space!" The others in the car thought he was kidding and they laughed, when, all of a sudden, three creatures came up from the side of the road in a single file. All four witnesses agree that they were shorter than a normal man and had very large heads with no hair and clay-like skin. They also noticed that their eyes were so huge that they covered most of the upper part of their heads. They had long slender arms, and all three were dressed in some type of dark tight-fitting suit.

At that point the witness on the driver's side shined the flashlight at the beings, and when the light hit their faces, the beings' eyes turned a deep red. The creatures then, as if frightened, turned around and ran down the hill through the thick brush as if it wasn't there. They then ran into what the witnesses describe as a "hole in the hill." Without warning, a giant triangular object with rows of multicolored lights appeared over the area where the beings vanished. The object was constructed of some type of very dark material and had one large amber light underneath. The witnesses said that this object was at least a hundred feet from end to end and was no more than several hundred feet from the ground. The object made no noise and then it slowly drifted toward them, all the while projecting a beam of light to the ground which finally engulfed their car. The light was so bright that it blinded the witnesses and they all indicated that they felt a tingling sensation up and down their backs.

The light went off, and when they looked out the car window to see if they could see where the object went, they were surprised that it was once again over the same area were they first saw it, then without warning it vanished as if someone had just turned out a light.

As soon as the object was gone the car started up (they tried it several times first), they then sped home and decided not to tell any one about the experience that they had. Stranger still, according to all four of them the encounter was less than a half hour, yet they arrived home several hours later than they should have. Were they abducted by aliens? Was the UFO using the chamber as a doorway to their world? Or was the missing time the product of time dilation effect, because they were in close proximity to the UFO as it bridged a pathway to another universe?

CHAPTER 9

The Paranormal Connection

*T*HE BALANCED ROCK IN North Salem, New York, lies just off Route 116. This road crosses near several reservoirs and has been the scene of a great number of Close Encounters with UFOs in Westchester County. The Balanced Rock is the largest dolmen (*dolmen* is an Irish word meaning "table stone") in the world, with the capstone weighing over forty tons. Dolmens were used as a marker to commemorate a great battle or the burial place of a powerful leader. Archaeologists have discovered that the dolmens in Ireland were used as burial tombs; however, no one is sure if anyone is buried under the great stone in North Salem, New York.

Near one end of the road lies the rock itself, and about eight miles away at the other end of the road is a chamber. We have heard a number of unusual stories concerning the Balanced Rock. People have reported strange cloaked figures seen surrounding the stone in the wee hours of the morning, only to suddenly disappear when approached. Some people who have taken photographs of the dolmen have reported globes of light which strangely appeared in their finished photos, objects they did not see while taking the photo. These globes of lights also have been reported to change position with each frame.

The dolmen is located on the largest known negative magnetic anomaly in New York state. People who visit the Balanced Rock report a very odd sensation when they touch a particular edge. Some have even become dizzy, disoriented, and have collapsed. The Balanced Rock is located at the focus of all the chambers that lie north of it. This means that if you draw straight lines on a map with all the chambers that are north of the Balanced Rock they will all line up with the huge North Salem dolmen. Whatever its purpose *really* is, there is no doubt that it is channeling and focusing some type of energy other than magnetic.

Ghost of a Druid Priest

A well-preserved chamber located just off Route 301 in Kent Cliffs, New York, also has a history of paranormal activity. This chamber is an oval-shaped double-capstone type with a high ceiling. It is made mostly of granite with fine quartz, with some shale and slate. Although the magnetic anomaly at this site has the lowest reading of all the chambers we have investigated, it has been the scene of some very strange reports. These reports include unseen forces and the sightings of unusual beings. Although there are quite a few people who have had experiences in this chamber we will relate the story, in his own words, of a local resident of Kent Cliffs, who we'll call Mike.

> I was taking a walk during the late part of the summer of 1992, when I passed by the chamber on 301. I knew about these things being there, but didn't know too much about them. I had lived in Kent Cliffs for about three years, and when I asked people about them I would get a number of different answers. These things are real spooky, especially at night. It was about 11 P.M. and it was very dark; a clear sky with no moon. I walked by the chamber and noticed a faint red glow coming from inside. I heard a sound that was like a soft electrical hum. I thought that someone was running some type of generator in there, so I crossed the street and walked through a short stretch of woods and entered the chamber.
>
> As soon as I entered, the red glow vanished along with the sound. I looked around and felt very uneasy, it was as if someone was watching me. You know the feeling, like you're in a dark cellar with someone down there with you, you can't see them but you know that you're not

alone. It wasn't more than thirty seconds when all of a sudden this force hits me. It was as if someone pushed me, I fell to the ground expecting to see someone standing there, but I saw no one at all!

As I laid there, I felt a presence, like someone was standing there. I slowly got up and was ready to run out of the damned thing when I was struck again, this time in the face. It felt like an invisible person was slapping me around. I was hit at least four times, and the last time I once again fell to the ground. I looked toward the opening and saw this figure of a man standing in the doorway. He was wearing a flowing white robe and had a long black beard with curly hair that hung over his shoulders. The thing that made me scared to death of him was his eyes. The eyes of this man were very dark, but the center of his pupils glowed and were a dull red color. He just stood there looking at me, when my eyes met his I could feel a tingling up and down my spine.

He then raised his hand and pointed his finger at me and the message I got from the look on his face was that I was to leave and not return. Although it was dark I could now see him plainly. I don't understand this, but it seemed as if he was glowing with a soft white halo around his body. The figure then dissolved into a cloud of white mist and then the mist was drawn into a nearby rock, just like there was a vacuum. The entire incident lasted about a minute or two. I then got up and ran out the chamber door. At night I still see the image of this guy in my sleep. Sometimes I wake up in the middle of the night in a cold sweat because I think he is waiting in the dark to take me away.

Although our investigation could find no evidence to support Mike's claim, we have no reason to doubt his story, since he has nothing to gain by reporting such an occurrence. Recently, psychic Loretta Chaney (see chapter 6, page 84), was taken to the area with no prior knowledge of Mike's story, or the history of the chamber. After several seconds in the chamber she exclaimed that the spirit of an individual was trying to contact her and when she described him, it matched the description of the entity that Mike saw. Loretta said that this spirit was trying to communicate with us, but was very worried about who we were and did not trust us. Her impression was that whoever or whatever this spirit was, he wanted us to leave.

Shortly after Mike's experience, a middle-aged woman and her teenage daughter visited the chamber on a Sunday afternoon. As the mother entered the chamber and slowly proceeded to the far left side of the wall, an invisible force struck her in the face, and knocked her to the dirt floor. She then screamed, and her daughter came running through the doorway, and as she entered she was also pushed back by some invisible force that pinned her against the far side of the right wall. As both women got to their feet, they heard a voice tell them, *"Get out!"* Both women then ran out, got into their car and never returned. When we interviewed the women, they were still terrified from the experience; the mother had a bruise on her left check that had not yet healed from the attack of the invisible assailant.

Two-Way Mirror to the Past

The next case is very similar to Mike's case because it involves the appearance of an identical being. Mike seemed to view the spirit of an earthbound Druid priest who interacted with him. In this case, however, the witness may actually have been viewing through four-dimensional space, into some time period in the past, and may have seen events that took place thousands of years ago. The witness (who we will shall refer to as Rob) had the luck or misfortune to purchase a house in Kent Cliffs, New York, with a stone chamber on his property. We present Rob's story in his own words.

> I had just bought the house here in Kent Cliffs, and I had this chamber in my backyard. I thought it would be convenient to use it for storage. I was worried though that the neighborhood dogs or even the kids might get in, so I decided to build a door. The day I picked to put the door in was a real hot day, and I was drinking a beer, but I only had one and I really don't think it had anything to do with what I saw. There I was, I had just stopped to take a break. I then sat down and looked out the chamber door, I was on the inside and I have to explain that there are woods right outside, so you can't see the house or anything. Well anyway, I had looked out and suddenly the air started to shimmer, like viewing something through heat-waves—everything was real distorted.

When it cleared I was no longer looking at my woods, but out onto a hill with a path coming down it and on the path I saw a group of men, perhaps seven or eight of them. These men looked like Vikings and they were dressed up in furs and some of them were wearing helmets with horns sticking out the top of them. They were being led by a man in a white gown who had long black curly hair. Then the air shimmered again and this time when it cleared I was no longer looking at the mountain side, but in a field. The man in the white robe was now standing right in front of the chamber entrance looking at me. By the look on his face he seemed just as startled to see me as I was to see him. So there we were just staring at each other for what seemed like an eternity, he then turned as if to talk to someone and the shimmering effect once again materialized in front of the door. Within a few seconds, the man and the unfamiliar scenery was gone and I was once again looking into the woods in my backyard.

The two cases above describing the Celtic-like figures are not isolated. In another incident a local researcher was walking out of a large chamber in Fahnestock Park, located in Putnam Valley, New York, when he had a similar experience. As he walked out of the chamber door, he glanced over to his right and saw several men walking down a path, holding shields and dressed in furs with horned helmets. The figures were about a hundred feet away and although he could not see the face of the trailing men, he noticed that the leader was very tall, and had a red beard. He couldn't believe his eyes, and turned away and shook his head. When he looked back, the figures were gone.

The Hooded Ones

We received a very bizarre report of an encounter with small, hooded, dwarf-like beings near the chamber on Reservoir Road in Southeast, New York. Before we begin this story, we must make note that this location has been the scene of several UFO reports, and a variety of paranormal phenomenon. The individuals involved belong to an organization in New York City that conducts paranormal research. Since Reservoir Road has had quite a few reports, members of this group frequently visit the area to see if anything unusual would occur. On most occasions they never experience anything abnormal, but during one spring night in 1992 they would have an encounter with the unknown that would leave them terrified for the rest of their lives.

They arrived at the location at about two in the morning and, as they stood on the lonely road, they began to hear what they described as "a buzzing sound." The noise seemed to be coming from a section of the road located near the stone chamber. One of the members of the group, a male in his late fifties, started walking toward the noise. The other members of the group tried to keep their flashlights trained on him as he slowly walked into the darkness.

Off to the right was a large outcrop of rock, he could still hear the noise and was sure that it was coming from inside the rock. As the others watched, they tried to call out to him because they had difficulty seeing him, as there was some type of distortion around the area. As he stood and stared at the rock, he went into a hypnotic, dream-like state, and was unable to move. As he watched the rock, it started to shimmer and it looked like a circle of blue water. Then out of the portal that had formed in the rock three dwarf-like, hooded beings walked out. The beings slowly walked toward him and, even though he was scared, he was unable to move. The three beings surrounded him and then, all at once, grabbed hold of him. They started pulling him toward the rock, and although his companions called out to him, he now felt very calm and wanted to go.

Then he realized what was happening and began to awaken from his trance-like state. He was still unable to break free from the dwarfs and was now being forcibly dragged to the portal in the rock. As the others ran down the road, they shined their lights on the beings. This seemed to frighten them, since they broke their grip, ran up the hill, merged with the rock, and disappeared. The researchers were so upset about what had taken place that they never returned to that location, and some of them quit investigating the paranormal.

A Similar Case

An incident that took place in Purchase, New York, was near a standing stone that appeared to have been carved into the shape of a rounded pillar with definite marks cut into it. The witness, a young student in his twenties, had gone to look at the stone during the night. He was standing near it when vertigo overcame him and caused him to fall to the ground against the rock.

When he looked up, he saw a number of dwarf-like creatures in hooded robes chanting and circling the stone. He reported to us that the noises they made sounded more like grunts from an animal rather than anything a human would make. He lost consciousness and when he woke up the hooded beings were gone and everything had become quiet.

FIGURE 9.1 Standing stone in Purchase, New York, on campus of the state university. Note markings.

There have been quite a few sightings of strange beings and creatures over the years around the chambers and the standing stones. The most common type are the hooded beings, and the gray, alien humanoids common in UFO reports. In some cases ancient Celts, Druids, and even Vikings have been seen. Are they ghosts, extraterrestrials, or "ultraterrestrials?" The chambers may actually act as a bridge to allow the past, present, and future to coexist together. The reports are too numerous to dismiss and they are made by people who would rather forget that their experiences took place.

The Fiery Spheres

Of all the reports of UFO-like phenomena around the chambers, the most common is of spherical lights that are no larger than a basketball. These lights seem to be under intelligent control or perhaps represent some unknown lifeform. One of the most interesting reports comes from Putnam county, New York, in which a young couple, John and Dotty Brendt had an encounter with the mysterious lights shortly after they moved into their new home. The incident as follows was told to us by John Brendt.

> When we bought the house, we first noticed the stone hut, but never thought much about it. The realtor told us that it was an old colonial root cellar, so I just left it at that. In 1984, my wife and I were awakened in the early hours of the morning by a strange buzzing sound. The sound was a pulsing one and sounded like some type of electrical generator. I looked out my window, which faces west, and saw a glow not far from the house. I thought there was a fire, so I got dressed and went outside. My wife tried to follow, but I told her to stay inside by the phone.
>
> As I walked toward the glow, the noise stopped. The night was very dark, so all I could see was this greenish glow. I began to realize that it was coming from the direction of the stone hut. As I approached the light changed from green, then to yellow and finally to a bright orange, then—without warning, the light vanished. My next thought was that there was somebody in there lighting a fire since the light was not very bright, just a soft glow. I stopped and tried to listen for voices, but it was quiet. I mean, it was *too quiet!*
>
> I can't remember the exact date, but it was during the last week of July. I did not venture into the woods because I did not have a flashlight, so I stopped about 150 feet from the stone hut. About ten seconds passed when I heard a sound, like paper ripping. The sound was so loud that I could feel it going through my body. Then three balls of gold light came out of the stone hut entrance and flew above the trees and just hovered there. I became frightened and started to walk back to the house. My wife put the outside [house] lights on,

and I could see her standing on the porch. The lights then jumped over the trees and dropped down to about five feet above the ground. They all moved together as if they were attached to a string. I started running back to the house and the lights slowly moved after me.

I joined my wife on the porch and the lights stopped about 100 feet or so from us and then they just hovered. They must have been there for about a good five minutes, then they split up. One turned red and shot straight up in the sky. The other two turned a deep amber and moved above our car, which was parked near the side of the house. The lights were about the size of basketballs, but they did not have a defined edge. The lights then changed to a rust color and began shooting sparks all over the place. At this point we went inside. I got on the telephone to call the police, but there was so much static that I could not even hear the dial tone. The lights outside began to glow brighter and brighter, and then, all of a sudden, the lightbulbs in the house—they just blew up! My wife started screaming and hid under the kitchen table. At that point the lights outside just started to fade until they vanished.

Our closest neighbor is about an eighth of a mile away, but they did not see anything. The next day I asked some people in the area about the stone huts and was surprised that nobody knew much about them. I then paid a visit to the museum in Pound Ridge, New York, to see if they had any information about the stone huts and started talking to an old gentleman who worked near the museum. I told him about the stone hut on the property and what happened. He listened politely and told me that people who live around these things have seen the same thing that my wife and I saw for over a hundred years. He remembers hearing stories about strange lights around the chambers from his grandfather. He said, according to legend, the chambers were built by the Druids who colonized the area over 4,000 years ago. The lights are said to be the captured spirits of Indians who the Druids priests captured and sacrificed in these chambers. This got me scared and when I went home I put a door on the stone hut. Since then, I have heard the sound again, but the lights never reappeared.

Case Analysis

We believe that the Brendt case is very well-documented and offers a great deal of information. The first sound that awoke the Brendts was a buzzing sound, which they compared to an electrical generator. Could this be some type of energy channeling through the walls of the chamber causing the quartz in it to resonate at a certain frequency? We heard about similar cases in which an electrical buzzing sound was heard, especially when some people put their ears up to the chamber walls. We believe that this buzzing sound is an energy pulse, possibly of electromagnetic origin which is used to activate the chamber.

The next thing Brendt reported was a color shift from green to yellow to bright orange. This represents a shift in the visible light spectrum from a high frequency to a low frequency. This frequency shift may be what is required to open up an interdimensional portal that is marked and controlled by the chamber. As the electromagnetic pulse reached the longer wavelengths it is possible that a chain reaction may take place to allow a doorway to open into another universe.

Brendt then heard a sound like the ripping of paper, a sound he felt going through his body. This represented energy emitted by the chamber beyond the frequency range of his eyes. As the hypothetical doorway opened, the spherical lights emerged from their universe to ours. Whether they are the actual travelers or not remains to be seen. We believe that an invisible alien intelligence emerges from this doorway and manifests itself in our world as the UFO phenomenon.

CHAPTER 10

The Path to Enlightenment

WE FEEL WE HAVE presented enough evidence to prove that the chambers are very old, and that a great deal of paranormal activity can be attributed to them. People continue to have otherworldly experiences in and around them, and the authors are no exception. We stated earlier that the chambers may mark doorways to another dimension. When this doorway is opened, objects or living things from this parallel reality may enter our world.

On the other hand, objects and living beings may also disappear from our reality into some close reality. Some of the chambers may be totally engulfed in this time-distortion effect and, when the field is activated, the entire chamber itself may vanish, and then reappear. In this case the chamber itself could act as a vehicle to transport people to this other world. Although to many this may sound a little far-fetched the authors may have actually seen it happen. The following incident describes this possibility, and to this day we can offer no reasonable explanation of what took place that late summer day in 1997.

We began looking for a number of chambers along a dirt road in Putnam county called Lockwood Lane. It was very warm and humid and we

125

had already hiked a considerable amount that day. We walked down the dirt road and found two chambers, so after we finished with them we began looking for a third, which was off the path into the woods. We had no idea were to look for it, but Marianne said that she had a sense or a feeling to check out a particular area. Phil agreed to follow Marianne because in the past her "feelings" had always proven correct. It was as if she sensed the energy generated from the chambers, and this often led her to the place where they were located. As we walked along the upper part of a path that circled a lake, we found the chamber—once again Marianne's feelings were correct!

We looked inside the chamber and it was typical of the other two we saw earlier. The only difference was that this one was filled with thousands of hungry mosquitoes. We took our measurements as quickly as possible, but no matter how fast we worked, we were still plagued by the insects. We left that chamber and noticed that there were two more listed on our map along the main trail, so we got back on the trail and continued to walk. As we walked on, we stared to looked to both sides of the trail, but there were no chambers. This was strange since, according to our map, they were located right along the side of the dirt road we were on. We finally reached the end of the unpaved part of Lockwood, and arrived at a gate that told us that we were at the residential area. We had gone too far, so we both sat down for a while and wondered how could we have missed them. After taking a short rest break and nourishing ourselves on wild berries, we decided to backtrack and rephotograph one of the first chambers we saw on Lockwood.

We then began to question the existence of the two chambers that were supposed to be on the side of the dirt trail, since we should have passed right by them. As we continued to walk we noticed a chamber on our left and we wondered if we went down a wrong trail, since it was not there when we first passed by this particular area. As we continued to walk we encountered another chamber also on the left. These were the two missing chambers that were not there when we passed earlier, but now they were there! Somehow the chambers were invisible when we passed them and now they reappeared!

FIGURE 10.1 The chamber located on Lockwood Lane.

We stopped to think about this and could find no explanation. We definitely passed the area earlier and the two chambers just were not there. We even noticed things around the chamber locations, like an old battery and a wire that was colored in red, that we saw before and noticed on the way back, so we knew we were in the same area. The only difference was when we first passed the location there were no chambers and now here they were! The only explanation is that the chambers actually vanished and were in this other dimension while we passed them and then reappeared later. We were quite amazed at what took place, but in spite of our excitement, we still took measurements of the two chambers and photographed them.

To list the number of people who have had paranormal experiences would be impossible for this book. Many of those who do visit the chambers or sleep in them overnight have more of a spiritual awakening. Such was the case of longtime Putnam County resident Martin Brech. Brech, a retired professor of philosophy, is also considered an

expert on the chambers. He gave us a great deal of assistance while
researching the material for this book.

Brech spent one night in the large chamber off Whangtown Road in
Kent Cliffs, New York. During the night he started feeling a sense of well-
being and saw himself surrounded by a glowing light. He then felt a presence while he was meditating and saw in his mind the figure of a being
standing behind him. The entity was shrouded in a robe with a hood and
gave off a great deal positive energy that made Brech feel very good and
at peace. Since then, Brech has returned to a number of the chamber sites
and experienced a great deal more. His mind has been opened up to the
universal intelligence and all of this has had a great influence on his life.
He told us that it would be almost impossible to describe the experience
in normal words, so he wrote the following piece.

> Allured, as ancestors in all ages everywhere, to seek awakening to
> nature's spirit in a sacred place of spiritual power, I explored her scat-
> tered remains of seclusion, finding a hilltop oak enfolding a standing
> stone again revealing nature's unfolding divinity composing our cos-
> mos as our sacred sanctuary.
>
> On this favored peak focusing her flowing spirit I learned to wait
> within her wounded womb of still barely retained silence and soli-
> tude. Here her fountain of spirit fostered my surrender, opening me
> to see and feel and be one with her and revealing her creative being
> in becoming as God unfolding in divine evolution.
>
> As some ancestors learned while many slept on, our full awaken-
> ing is our essential experience, stripping all our shells, in spiritual
> rebirth, opening us to our world's unfolding miracle seen truly and
> fully for the first time. A vision we see only when beyond mere look-
> ing, without which people and planet perish in vain.
>
> Upon our opening all re-appears bathed in a luminous and gentle
> grace, often first seen flowing from a primal focus within our once
> and now again primeval home: as from this solitary, sky-embracing
> huge hilltop oak firmly hugging a numinous stone that stands erect.
>
> Enticed by this embrace of its standing stone it clasps in its cleav-
> age of thigh-like roots, I bow and sit and reach out to touch the
> trunk of this hill—crowning surge of stately oak, while my finger
> held above its phallic stone feels a flow of earth's energy enter me
> bestowing its harmony enthralling me.

Fully absorbed in reverential awe, a vision of wholeness softly envelops me, with the sensuous and the sacred again blending into our timeless experience of our holy oneness. I dissolve into the blissful glow of spirit and all as one is now seen eternally bathed in the blessedness of God's-Being-In-Becoming. May our spiritual oneness of being be our experience and not merely be our belief or concept or be rejected by minds content to be solely analytic.

There is no doubt that the above passage was inspired by being in an area that contains a great deal of spiritual power. Brech is but one of dozens who, while in a chamber or near one of the standing stones, have felt a rejuvenation of spirit. We believe that thoughts, ideas, feelings, and knowledge can be contained in an energy field. It is very possible that the ancient knowledge of long ago is still held in the chambers, and to access this information one has to let go of one's conscious mind. We also feel that a certain amount of the information for this book was obtained the same way.

At one time, the chambers were used as a path to enlightenment. Today, with all the construction around them and the negative thoughts of our world, their power has diminished, but they are still potent generators of energy. Unfortunately, most of these ancient sacred sites are not protected and they are slowly being destroyed. We hope that our continued research will educate and open the minds of others to aid in their preservation. We also feel that we have found the chambers' true purpose and place in history, and to us they are no longer lost in time.

APPENDIX 1

Contacts

*T*HE AUTHORS PLAN REGULAR tours of the chambers. If you are interested in seeing some of them, please write to us at: P.O. Box 4218, Greenwich, CT 06831, or e-mail us at: pimbrogn@windwardny.org. We also offer photographs and video of the locations for those of you who can not come to the east coast of the United States. All proceeds are used to continue our research and help save these sites for the future. Below are other contacts that may interest our readers.

The Gungywamp Society
    David Barron, President
    E-mail: Noank2@aol.com
    334 Brook Street
    Noank, CT 06340
    (860) 536-2887

Early Sites Research Society
    Long Hill
    Rowley, MA 01969
    (508) 948-2410

America's Stonehenge
  P.O. Box 84
  North Salem, NH 03073
  (603) 893-8300
  Web site: www.stonehengeusa.com

Loretta Chaney
  304 Federal Road
  Suite 204
  Brookfield, CT 06804
  (203) 730-0600
  E-mail: Lchny22@aol.com

NEARA, Hudson Valley, NY
  Martin Brech
  36 Brookdale Rd.
  Mahopac, NY 10541

NEARA, Vermont
  Donna Martin
  Box 150, Wildcat Rd.
  Chittenden, VT 05737

NEARA, New Hampshire
  Colgate Gilbert, III
  P.O. Box 1152
  Keene, NH 03431

NEARA, Connecticut and Rhode Island
  Richard Lynch
  12 Greenbriar Rd.
  Greenville, RI 02828

NEARA, Massachusetts
    Betty Peterson
    2 Oxford Place
    Worcester, MA 01609

Temenos
    65 Mt. Mineral Road
    Shutesbury, MA 01702

Chamber Information
    Phil Imbrogno
    P.O. Box 4218
    Greenwich, CT 06831
    E-mail: pimbrogn@windwardny.org

APPENDIX 2

Tables and Charts

*T*HE RESEARCH WE UNDERTOOK on this project over the years has been like a great adventure. We had to go back in time, imagine the way things were over 2,000 years ago, place ourselves in that time period, and ask why! The work that produced this book began in 1982 and is still continuing today. We feel we have presented a convincing argument that the chambers were built by ancient European explorers, who came to the northeast United States as far back as the Bronze Age. We have also discovered that the chambers and nearby standing stones generate a great deal of energy over a broad frequency range. This energy opens and closes a door to another dimension, and is the source of a great deal of paranormal activity in southern New York.

In this section, we present graphs and tables so that our readers can appreciate the extent of the research that we have accomplished over the years. After fourteen years of collecting information, we had quite a bit of data and it was now time to make sense of it all. We put together fourteen data study sheets that include charts, graphs, and tables. The following will explain each of the study sheets and interpret the data.

Table 1: Physical Characteristics of the Chambers

This table shows the raw chamber data. The **Location** is given either by a road or, if the chamber is not on a road, by the name of the area. For example, Ninham and Fahnestock are state parks in Putnam County, New York. The **Length, Width,** and **Height** of the chamber is given in inches. **C. Slab #** stands for the number of stones used to make the roof of the chamber. **Compass** denotes the number of degrees on the compass: 0 or 360 is due north, 90 is east, 180 is south, and 270 is west. **Type** is the shape of the chamber. There are two types: *Oval,* which can be squarish or round, and *Gallery,* which are cylindrical or rectangular in shape. The **Purpose** stands for our hypothesis of the use of the chamber. **Markings** indicate if we found any etchings in the rock in the chamber or nearby. **C. Stones** indicates if we found any standing stones, or stones that have been carved in or around the chamber. **Activity** indicates the type of paranormal phenomena reported in, or within a short distance from, the chamber. This activity is listed as: strange lights, ghosts, UFO and UFO-like phenomena, and psychic experiences, which can include telepathic messages, visions, and other forms of extrasensory perception (ESP). Also other listings include energy in the form of electromagnetic bursts and magnetic anomalies (deviations on the compass that can have the effect of disorientating animals and humans). Unknown factors are listed as "Unkn."

Location	Length	Width	Height	C. Slab #	Compass	Type	Purpose	Markings	C. Stones	Activity
Ninham Mt	203	85	61	72	40	Gallery	Burial	Yes	Yes	UFO
Fahnestock	294	116	67	12	240	Gallery	Ritual	Yes	Yes	Lights
Fahnestock	161	103	67	7	220	Oval	Burial	Yes	Yes	Psychic
Rt. 301	190	101	81	7	120	Gallery	Shelter	No	No	None
Rt. 301	194	120	64	7	90	Oval	Ritual	Yes	Yes	Paranormal
Rt. 301	191	139	83	6	166	Oval	Ritual	No	Yes	Paranormal
Whangtown	319	110	75	10	220	Gallery	W. Solstice	No	No	Psychic
Whangtown	190	45	46	7	220	Gallery	Solstice	No	No	None
Oscawana	163	68	62	5	180	Gallery	Shelter	No	Yes	Psychic
Oscawana	258	102	80	7	180	Gallery	Shelter	No	Yes	Psychic
Rt. 164	246	173	80	9	20	Oval	Shelter	No	No	None
Putnam Lake	312	145	96	Unkn.	180	Gallery	Unkn.	No	No	Unkn.
Peach Lake	Unkn.	47	59	Unkn.	230	Gallery	Unkn.	No	No	Psychic
Dixon Rd.	223	109	77	6	80	Gallery	Solstice	No	No	None
Lockwood	130	49	63	4	160	Gallery	Shelter	No	No	None
Lockwood	223	64	65	6	160	Gallery	Shelter	No	No	None
Lockwood	144	72	62	6	180	Gallery	Shelter	No	No	None
Lockwood	192	77	65	7	190	Gallery	Shelter	No	No	None
Lockwood	125	61	62	6	240	Gallery	Unkn.	No	No	None
Cole Shears	220	118	75	7	60	Gallery	Unkn.	No	No	UFO
Cole Shears	165	128	81	7	75	Oval	Ritual	Yes	Yes	UFO

TABLE 1 Physical Characteristics of the Chambers.

Location	Length	Width	Height	C. Slab #	Compass	Type	Purpose	Markings	C. Stones	Activity
Ninham Rd.	288	112	74	7	90	Gallery	Shelter	No	No	UFO
Ludington	188	72	65	6	240	Gallery	Astronomical	No	No	None
Ludington	160	54	56	4	240	Gallery	Astronomical	No	No	None
Ludington	160	60	56	6	140	Gallery	Unkn.	No	No	None
Ludington	175	60	54	7	240	Gallery	Astronomical	No	No	None
Ludington	151	91	61	6	240	Gallery	Astronomical	No	No	None
White Pond	Unkn.	Unkn.	Unkn.	6	140	Oval	Ritual	No	No	UFO
Rushmore	230	122	80	7	300	Gallery	Storage	No	No	None
Peekskill #1	211	112	75	6	140	Gallery	Solstice	No	No	None
Peekskill #2	175	75	68	7	220	Gallery	Solstice	No	No	None
Peekskill #3	174	118	58	4	140	Gallery	Unkn.	No	No	None
Tinker Hill	145	60	75	6	145	Gallery	Unkn.	No	No	Spook Light
Barger	288	89	78	7	105	Gallery	Solstice?	No	Yes	Ghost
Kramers	222	114	78	7	140	Gallery	Unkn.	No	No	None
Bell Hollow	216	99	65	6	166	Gallery	Shelter	No	No	None
Canopus	132	120	76	2	130	Oval	Ritual	Yes	Yes	Psychic
Bullet Hole	196	49	74	7	90	Gallery	Solstice	No	No	None
Icepond	153	85	55	5	340	Gallery	Storage	No	No	None
Fahnestock	158	117	Unkn.	Unkn.	120	Gallery	Collapsed	No	No	Lights
Fahnestock	150	145	Unkn.	Unkn.	220	Gallery	Collapsed	No	No	Lights
Allview Rd.	Unkn.	Unkn.	Unkn.	Unkn.	140	Gallery	Unkn	No	No	None
Indian Brook	158	76	67	6	110	Gallery	Solstice?	No	No	Energy?

Location	Length	Width	Height	C. Slab #	Compass	Type	Purpose	Markings	C. Stones	Activity
Sterling Lake	172	123	72	6	120	Square	Ritual	No	Yes	UFO
Wixson Pond	209	108	68	6	210	Gallery	Astronomical	No	No	None
Rt. 6	212	125	84	6	140	Gallery	Unkn.	No	No	None
Washington	110	72	64	2	140	Oval	Unkn.	No	No	None
Ludington Rd.	170	90	95	6	200	Oval	Ritual	Yes	Yes	Ghost
Whangtown	144	103	77	4	140	Oval	Ritual	Yes	Yes	Psychic
Barger St. #1	Unkn.	Unkn.	Unkn.	Unkn.	120	Unkn.	Astronomical	No	Yes	Unkn.
Barger St. #2	339	108	85	7	120	Gallery	Astronomical	No	No	None
Rochdale	297	109	79	10	120	Gallery	Astronomical	No	Yes	None
Barger #3	303	110	74	8	130	Gallery	Astronomical	No	No	Lights
Barger #4	252	100	75	4	140	Gallery	Astronomical	No	Yes	None
Bryant Pond	144	105	75	3	90	Oval	Equinox	No	No	None
Tinker Hill	216	112	75	4	140	Gallery	Unkn.	No	No	Energy?
Peekskill #4	Unkn.	Unkn.	Unkn.	Unkn.	130	Unkn.	Unkn.	Unkn.	Unkn.	Unkn.
Peekskill #5	145	90	66	6	140	Oval	Unkn.	Yes	Yes	UFO
Agor #1	239	86	75	6	300	Gallery	Set Sun	No	No	Anomaly
Agor#2	229	82	75	6	130	Gallery	Unkn.	No	Yes	None
Agor#3	154	76	92	6	130	Gallery	Unkn.	No	No	None
Loos Lane	154	103	76	7	110	Gallery	Equinox	No	No	None
Oscawana#1	202	100	74	6	290	Gallery	Set Sun	No	No	UFO
Oscawana#2	266	120	80	7	350	Gallery	Ritual	Yes	Yes	UFO
Reservoir	186	100	93	6	180	Gallery	Ritual	No	Yes	UFO/Psychic

TABLE 1 (continued) Physical Characteristics of the Chambers.

Table 2: Celtic/Christian Calendar Holidays

This table can be used to compare Celtic ritual days with various phenomena presented throughout the book. It should also be used for charts 3, 5, and 6.

DATE	CELTIC HOLIDAY	CHRISTIAN HOLIDAY
November 1	Samhain	All Saints' Day
December 22	Alban Arthuan	Winter Solstice
February 2	Brigantia	Candlemass
March 21	Alban Eiler	Vernal Equinox
May 1	Beltaine	May Day
June 22	Alban Heruin	Summer Solstice
August 1	Lugnassadh	Lammas
September 23	Alban Elved	Autumnal Equinox
October 29–November 1	Ruis	Hallowe'en

TABLE 2 Celtic Calendar listing holidays and Christian counterparts.

Chart 1: Cases of High Strangeness

This study analyzes a total of 311 cases from 1980 to 1996, and lists them by the city or town that they took place in. By definition, a High Strangeness case is one that is far more unusual than a typical UFO sighting. These cases include: the appearance of strange beings and creatures, Close Encounters of the Third and Fourth Kind, contact experiences, strange sounds and lights, and poltergeist phenomena.

We found from the study that the majority of these High Strangeness cases took place in the town of Kent Cliffs, New York, which also has the greatest number of chambers. Nearby Putnam Valley, New York, is the area of the second greatest number of reports, it also has the second greatest number of chambers. The study shows that there is a relationship to the number of chambers and standing stones in an area and the frequency of paranormal phenomena.

Chart 2: Percentage of Paranormal Cases

This chart divides each type of paranormal phenomena into percentages. We see (which was no surprise to us) that the most frequent paranormal event reported is an encounter with a UFO. Remember these are High Strangeness cases and the UFO activity is of the close encounter or contact type. The center of the UFO activity was once again in Kent Cliffs, New York, where there is the greatest number of chambers.

Electromagnetic Effects, or **EM:** Unusual interference on radio or television, electrical power surges in the area, unexplained blackouts, failure of automobile electrical ignition, appliances in homes turning off and on for no apparent reason, and electrostatic discharges similar to lightning.

Lights: These are reports of globes of light that do not behave like electrical phenomena. They are similar to the "spook light" reports of Ireland, Scotland, and Marfa, Texas. They are usually blue, yellow, or white in color, and sometimes are seen going in and out of a large UFO that is moving slowly or hovering in the sky. An example of this type of phenomenon is the spook light of Reservoir Road described in detail in chapter 8.

Strange Sounds: Include those sounds that are unusual, but are audible to the human ear. They can be a steady tone or beeps of various frequencies. Hissing, scratching, and grinding sounds have also been reported. These sounds have often been heard before a UFO or other similar type of phenomena is witnessed.

Creatures: The sighting of a unknown living organism around a chamber area. This may include UFO-type beings, Bigfoot-like creatures, dwarfs, or any type of being that is not indigenous to our plane of reality. Although there aren't too many reports of strange creatures, the cases that we have are interesting and are covered in detail in chapter 8.

Ghosts, and *Ghost-related phenomena:* This includes the appearance of phantom-like entities. Some of the reports include the ghosts of Druid priests and Celtic warriors. Ghosts from the Revolutionary War and the spirits of Native Americans have also been reported in and around a chamber location. If the chambers are portals to another reality, then it is not surprising that these events have been reported over and over again. What *is* surprising is that reports of ghosts and spirits make up the smallest percentage of all.

Poltergeist: These reports include physical objects that disappear and reappear, or objects that move around with no visible physical cause. These reports also include unseen forces that have pushed, hit, or touched people at the chamber sites. For example, the large oval chamber on Route 301 in Kent Cliffs, New York, has had several reports of people being physically assaulted by some unseen force. The chamber off Reservoir Road in Southeast, New York, is one of several structures that have a history of this type of paranormal occurrence.

Psychic Phenomena: This includes a variety of psychic phenomena. Some of the most common examples are people hearing voices, telepathic messages, visions, and cases of enhanced extrasensory perception. In a number of the chambers, some people who already have psychic abilities seem to have their power increased and have been able to see into the past and future and obtain a great amount of data about the chambers and their builders.

UFOs: The UFO phenomena makes up the majority of the reported paranormal cases. Perhaps it is true that the intelligence behind the UFOs has, in fact, taken over the chambers, and now uses them for traveling between their dimension and ours.

Chart 3: Relation of Rising Sun to Solstice Chamber Doors

This graph shows the declination of the sun in relation to the opening of the chamber at the Whangtown Road site in Kent Cliffs, New York. The dates on the graph are all important days on the Celtic calendar. (For a detailed explanation see table 2 and chapter 4.) The top part of the graph represents the "light" part of the year (spring and summer). This is when the sun's vertical ray is north of the equator. The bottom of the graph represents the "dark" half of the year (fall and winter) when the sun's vertical ray is below the equator. Notice that the angle in degrees of the sun above and below the celestial equator for the light and dark half of the year is the same number of degrees. For example, the declination of the rising sun as seen from the inside of the chamber during the first day of winter (December 22) is -25 degrees, while the declination of the rising sun as seen from the inside of the chamber during the first day of summer (June 22) is +25 degrees.

There is no doubt that this chamber was built and designed not only to tell the time of the solstice, but also the other important holidays. However, we could not find any evidence that this chamber was used to tell the time of the equinoxes, since on both dates the sun is directly on the celestial equator. A second chamber located within walking distance from this chamber may have been used for this purpose since its orientation is 90 degrees. Ninety degrees represents half a hemisphere, which would align the chamber's opening to the declination of the sun on the celestial equator. This would mean that on March 22 and September 22 the sun would rise due east, which is the exact orientation of the door of this smaller chamber.

Chart 4: EMP at Chamber Site

If some of the chambers do mark the locations of a doorway to a parallel reality, then it is possible, in theory, that when the "door" swings open, a burst of energy might flow into our universe. The same might happen when the door is shut closed. It's like a door that opens from the outside on a cold winter day. When the door is opened, a burst of cold air enters the home; when the door is closed, a slam can be heard. Perhaps when the door to this other dimension is opened and closed, two different types of energy are released into our world. We mentioned earlier that evidence suggest that UFOs might be using certain chambers to travel from their world to ours. This would explain why there is an outbreak of paranormal activity before and after a series of UFO sightings. The energy released by the opening and closing the dimensional door may be the power source to trigger the paranormal events. In theory, part of this energy should be generated as an electromagnetic pulse (EMP). This pulse should be picked up on a radio receiver that has the ability to scan a multitude of frequencies in a short amount of time.

During the fall of 1997, we were able to borrow a receiver that was able to scan frequencies between 16 MHz and 2,000 MHz. An oscilloscope and a chart recorder were also used. We picked the oval chamber on Route 301 since it has had a history of paranormal events. We decided to monitor the frequencies at night, so we began the experiment at 11 P.M. We continued to scan for two hours, then at 1:15 A.M. on September 21, we picked up a pulse that started around 16.50 MHz, and peaked at 1,675 MHz in the microwave region. The pulse continued and started to drop in signal strength after 1,700, and continued to drop until we lost it at 2,000 MHz. We could find no explanation for the energy burst. Was it a doorway to another universe opening and closing? Much to our dismay, we received no reports of UFO sightings or any other type of paranormal activity in that area, but that does not mean they did not take place. It could mean that they were just not reported!

Chart Strip of Electromagnetic Pulse

This chart (Figure A, below) shows the EMP for chamber number two on Route 301 in Kent Cliffs, New York, made on November 1, 1997 at 4 hours and 38 minutes Universal Time (11:38 EST). The recording indicates a strong electromagnetic signature at 1,675 MHz. This pulse may have been used at one time to open and close the doorways to a parallel universe.

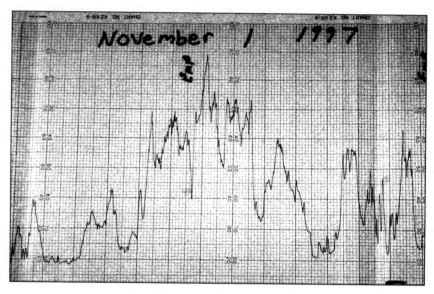

FIGURE A   EMP recording at Chamber 2, Route 301, Kent Cliffs, New York.

Chart 5: Paranormal Cases by Month

This chart plots the number of cases that occur during the year. Once again the study was based on 311 cases from 1980–1996. We see an increase in reports between February and March, another smaller peak in July and finally one last peak in October. The difference in the October peak when compared to the other peak months is that the decline in the number of reports is more gradual. Interestingly, each peak is on, or very close to, the holy days on the Celtic calendar (see Table 2). Also note that there are *three* major peaks, a number that the Celts held sacred.

Chart 6: Time and Paranormal Activity

This graph charts the time paranormal activity took place. We see a peak at three in the morning, and a high peak at eight in the evening. This graph is very similar to our study showing the time of UFO events throughout the world, found in our first book, *Contact of the 5th Kind*.

Charts 7, 8, and 9: Magnetic Anomaly Studies

Paranormal researchers have always suspected a connection between magnetic anomalies and various phenomena, especially UFOs. A magnetic anomaly is an increase or decease in the magnetic field of the Earth. At first we thought we would see an *increase* in the anomaly, but were very surprised when our results showed a negative anomaly. The Earth's magnetism seems to be focused at the site by a chamber or standing stone, and then channeled off into somewhere else. The overlay of each study shows a huge dip in the magnetic field of the Earth as you approach the site location. The magnetic energy is then focused sharply into a funnel-like shape, then it vanishes—but to where? It is possible that the energy is being sucked into a parallel universe by a four-dimensional vortex. This may be the location where a portal opens up from this nearby dimension into ours. The energy may be used to open and close the portal "door."

Chart 7: The Balanced Rock. The balanced rock showed the largest anomaly, which was focused toward the left side of the boulder. The reading was -400 less than normal magnetic readings. People who have stood in this area have often complained of feeling pressure, or have become disorientated.

Chart 8: The double chamber off Oscawana Road in Putnam Valley, New York, showed the second largest anomaly. Once again, the profile is in the shape of a vortex, and this energy may be funnelled into this other dimension to act as a power source to warp space to open and close the portal. The reading here was -320, and there was a compass deviation of over 160 degrees. The diagram also shows what the magnetic profile would be like if the anomaly were removed.

Chart 9: The oval chamber on Route 301 in Kent Cliffs, New York. This had one of the lowest readings (about -90), and was focused toward the outside of the chamber entrance. It is possible that whatever was used to cause the anomaly was removed when the road was dug up and widened. The magnetic anomaly study proves that the chambers and some of the standing stones were used to channel the Earth's natural energy. We would like to thank Dr. Bruce Cornet who conducted the study, and we conclude with his remarks in a letter to Phil sent shortly after the anomaly research was completed.

> Thank you for including me on your field trip to the stone chambers in Westchester and Putnam counties last Sunday. I hope that we can return to some of the chambers for a more detailed magnetic survey before I have to return the magnetometer. I prepared three diagrams of my magnetic survey for two stone chambers and the Balanced Rock. The Balanced Rock anomaly is the strongest at about -400 gammas, while the Kent Cliffs stone chamber is the weakest at -88 gammas. All three anomalies appear to be too sharp and confined to be natural. A colleague of mine said that he suspects some cultural object buried underneath the chambers may be responsible. He told me that he found similar anomalies over old oil well casings. But the distinction is that oil-well casings do not reverse the Earth's magnetic field.
>
> At the Putnam Valley School chamber, I took all my readings relative to the compass, which I thought was pointing to the true direction of magnetic north. When I completed my map and compared it to the road/ topographic map, I discovered that the north direction at the center of the anomaly was almost the reverse of the Earth's north direction. North direction at the anomaly is oriented along the

vertical set of measurements and toward the top of the page, and is about 160 degrees to the south southwest of magnetic north. For an object to do that requires four conditions:

1. It is very magnetic and close to the surface.
2. It has a magnetic dipole that is nearly reversed compared to the current magnetic field of Earth.
3. It has its south pole oriented upwards.
4. It is oriented nearly vertical with a slight inclination to the south-southwest in order to give a south southwest direction for the compass north arrow.

It is highly unlikely, therefore that whatever is causing the extreme anomaly at the Putnam Valley stone chamber is natural. Perhaps someone drilled a well hole there and left an iron casing or drill pipe in the hole. If that is unlikely, then there is something close to the surface that needs to be excavated. If it dates back to the time the stone chamber was constructed, it will be very significant, not to mention interesting. If it is manmade and more recent, then we need to check other stone chambers for similar objects. A metal detector will also work to verify the anomaly.

Chart 10: Chamber Opening Orientation

This graph shows the opening of sixty-five chambers to their direction on the compass. The majority of chambers face to the southeast and west. This seems like a logical decision for their construction, since these chambers would catch the sun in the morning and late afternoon. Chambers facing due east or west may be equinox chambers, while chambers facing north may have been used for religious ceremonies.

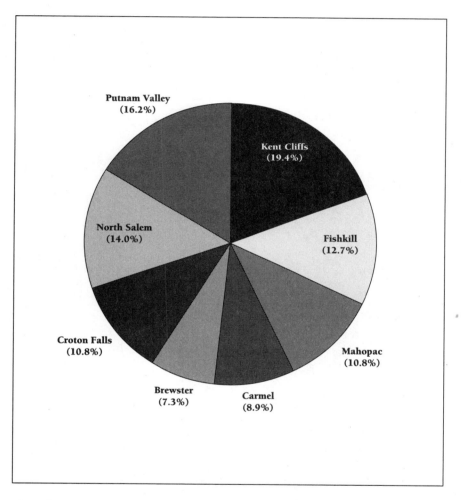

CHART 1   Cases of "High Strangeness." (All towns located in New York state, and based on a total of 311 cases.)

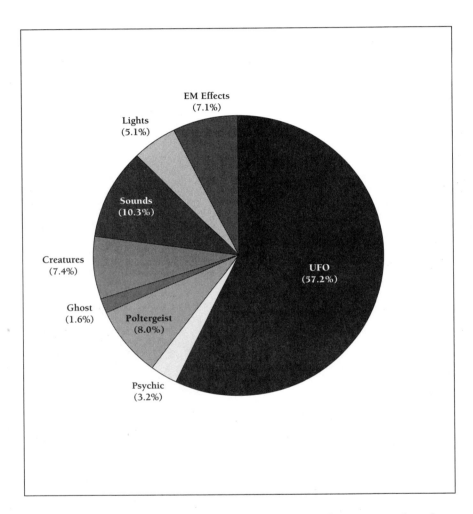

CHART 2   Percentages of Paranormal Cases. Type and percentage based on 311 total cases (All locations Westchester, Putnam, and Dutchess counties, New York state).

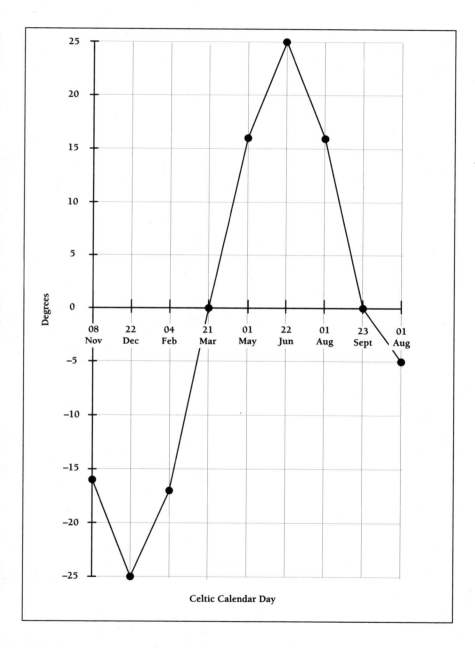

CHART 3   Declination of the rising sun through door of Solstice Chamber, Whangtown Road, Kent Cliffs, New York.

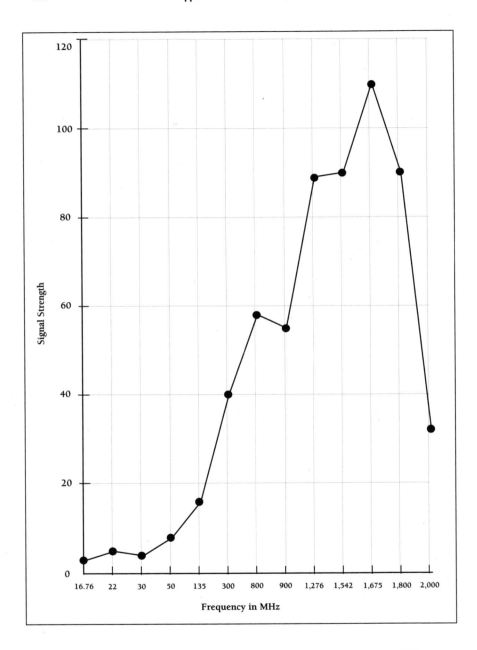

CHART 4   EMP at chamber site (Route 301 Chamber at Kent Cliffs, New York).

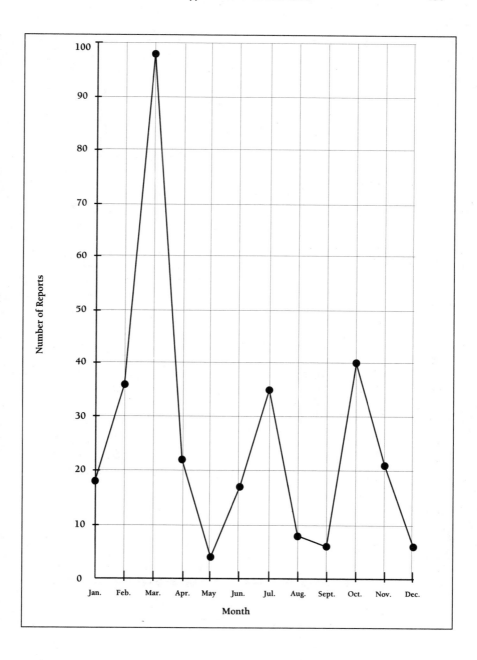

CHART 5   Paranormal cases by month (based on a total of 311 cases).

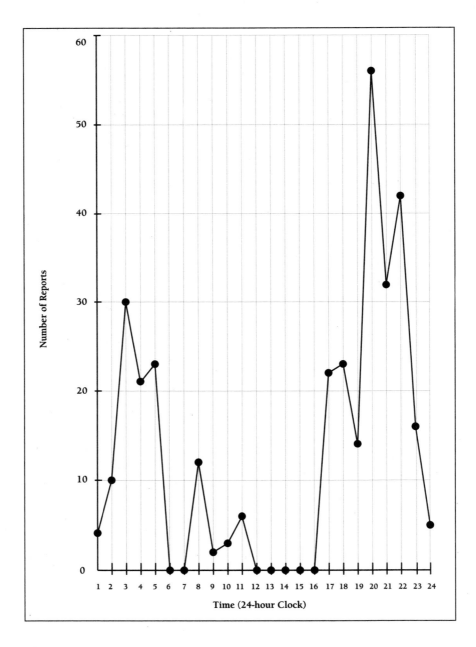

Chart 6   Time of Day and Paranormal Activity (near chambers, based on a total of 311 cases).

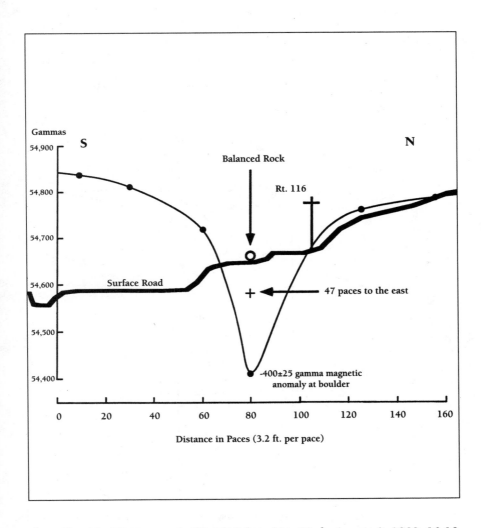

CHART 7 Magnetic anomaly (North Salem, New York, August 2, 1992, 10:13 A.M.).

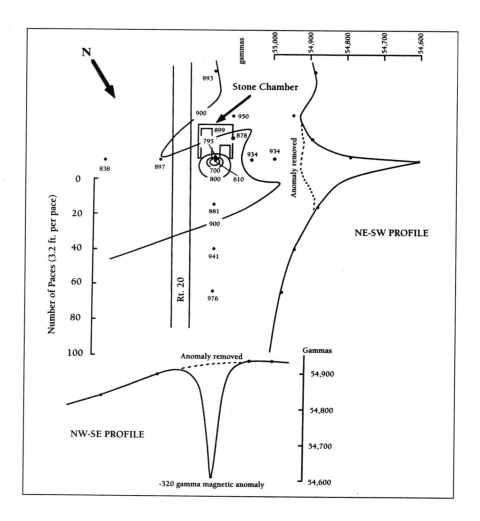

CHART 8   Magnetic anomaly (North Salem, New York, August 2, 1992, 3:08 P.M.).

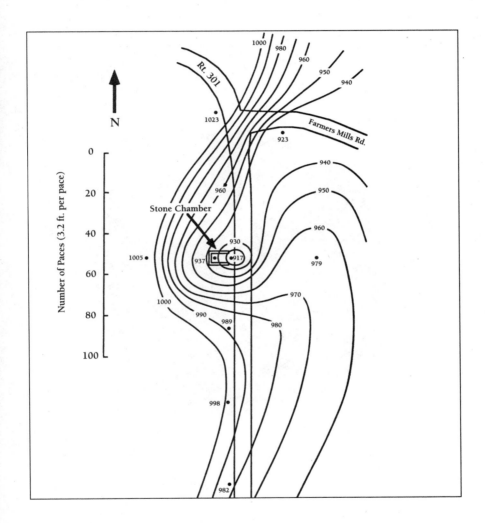

CHART 9   Magnetic anomaly (Kent Cliffs, New York, August 2, 1992).

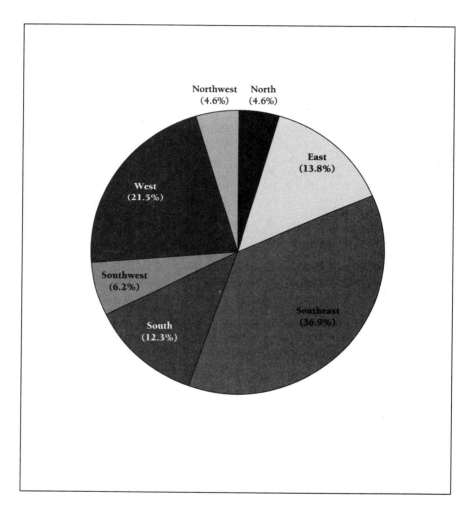

CHART 10   Chamber opening orientation (based on 65 chambers).

INDEX

fairies, 53, 107

Feder, Dr. Ken, 37

Fell, Dr. Barry, 6, 11, 32, 77, 81, 117

Fishkill, 59, 97, 149

Freemason Society, 94–95

Funk, Dr. Robert, 37–38

G

ghosts (in relation to chambers), 5, 53, 108–109, 116, 138–139, 150

Greeks, 17–18, 51, 53, 89

Gundestrup cauldron, 62

Gungywamp Society, The, 31, 35, 131

H

Hades, 53

Hallowe'en, 41

Hecataeus, 51

"High Strangeness" cases, 4–6, 141, 149

Holy Roman Empire, 10

Holy Trinity, 44, 53

Horrigan, Jack Allen, 91–94

Horrigan, Marianne, 34, 45, 62, 91, 126

Hudson River Valley, 59, 69

Hudson Valley, New York, UFO case, 1–7, 26, 62, 69, 71, 80–82, 112, 114, 119, 121, 124, 136–139, 141–144, 146, 150

I

Imbolc, 55

K

Kent Cliffs, New York, 4–6, 17, 38, 42, 44, 62, 96, 116, 118, 128, 141–143, 145, 147, 149, 151–152, 157

King's Chamber, 99–101

☽ REACH FOR THE MOON

Llewellyn publishes hundreds of books on your favorite subjects! To get these exciting books, including the ones on the following pages, check your local bookstore or order them directly from Llewellyn.

ORDER BY PHONE
- Call toll-free within the U.S. and Canada, 1-800-THE MOON
- In Minnesota, call (651) 291-1970
- We accept VISA, MasterCard, and American Express

ORDER BY MAIL
- Send the full price of your order (MN residents add 7% sales tax) in U.S. funds, plus postage & handling to:

  Llewellyn Worldwide
  P.O. Box 64383, Dept. K357-3
  St. Paul, MN 55164–0383, U.S.A.

POSTAGE & HANDLING
(For the U.S., Canada, and Mexico)
- $4.00 for orders $15.00 and under
- $5.00 for orders over $15.00
- No charge for orders over $100.00

We ship UPS in the continental United States. We ship standard mail to P.O. boxes. Orders shipped to Alaska, Hawaii, The Virgin Islands, and Puerto Rico are sent first-class mail. Orders shipped to Canada and Mexico are sent surface mail.

International orders: Airmail—add freight equal to price of each book to the total price of order, plus $5.00 for each non-book item (audio tapes, etc.).

Surface mail—Add $1.00 per item.

Allow 2 weeks for delivery on all orders.
Postage and handling rates subject to change.

DISCOUNTS
We offer a 20% discount to group leaders or agents. You must order a minimum of 5 copies of the same book to get our special quantity price.

FREE CATALOG

Get a free copy of our color catalog, *New Worlds of Mind and Spirit.* Subscribe for just $10.00 in the United States and Canada ($30.00 overseas, airmail). Many bookstores carry *New Worlds*—ask for it!

Visit our web site at www.llewellyn.com for more information.

Contact of the Fifth Kind

The silent invasion has begun.
What the government has covered up

Philip J. Imbrogno &
Marianne Horrigan

George and Maria have a daughter who is almost two years old. One day she brought out her doll and asked her mom to open its head. Maria asked her where she had seen something like that and she told her mom, "They do it to daddy at night."

How would the people of this country react if they knew that their government allowed an alien intelligence to abduct them and experiment on them in exchange for technological advances?

Contact of the Fifth Kind is a new approach to UFO research that is filled with hundreds of documented alien contact and abduction cases. Philip J. Imbrogno is one of the few researchers who actually goes out into the field to personally investigate the evidence. And the evidence, in some cases, is so overwhelming that even the most skeptical of readers will not be able to deny that there is an intelligence currently interacting with certain people on this planet.

1-56718-361-1, 256 pp., 5 3/16 x 8, softcover   **$9.95**

Night Siege

The Hudson Valley UFO Sightings

Dr. J. Allen Hynek,
Philip J. Imbrogno & Bob Pratt

In 1983, just a few miles north of New York City, hundreds of suburbanites were startled to see something hovering in the sky. They described it as a series of flashing lights that formed a "V," as big as a football field, moving slowly and silently.

It has been seen many times since then, yet the media has remained silent about it, as has the military, the FAA, and the nation's scientists. Now, in *Night Siege,* expert UFO investigators reveal the amazing evidence that cannot be denied and the more than 7,000 sightings that cannot be dismissed.

A classic in the field, *Night Siege* has been called one of the best researched and factual UFO books to date. This second edition is revised and expanded with sightings up to 1995.

1-56718-362-X, 288 pp., 5 ³⁄₁₆ x 8, 8-pp. b&w photo insert $9.95

Atlantis

Insights from a Lost Civilization

Shirley Andrews

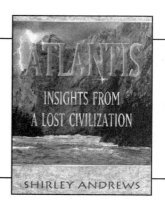

The legend of lost Atlantis turns to fact as Shirley Andrews uniquely correlates a wealth of information from more than 100 classical and Atlantean scholars, scientists and psychics to describe the country and its inhabitants.

Review the scientific and geological evidence for an Atlantic continent, which refutes the popular notion that Atlantis was located in the Mediterranean. Follow the history of Atlantis from its beginnings to its destruction, and see a portrait of Atlantean society: its religion, architecture, art, medicine, and life style. Explore shamanism, the power of crystals, ancient healing techniques, pyramid energy, ley lines, the influence of extraterrestrials and the origin of the occult sciences. Learn what happened to the survivors of Atlantis, where they migrated, and how the survivors and their descendants made their mark on cultures the world over.

1-56718-023-X, 272 pp., 6 x 9, illus., softcover　　　　　　　$12.95

Mysteries of the Deep

Amazing Phenomena in
Our World's Waterways

Compiled by Frank Spaeth

I snapped a look out the window. The right wing had simply disappeared from sight! It was an eerie feeling, as though we'd flown into some impossible limbo. I then noticed that what had been blue sky had changed to a creamy yellow, as though we were in the middle of a bottle of eggnog.
　　　　　　　　　　　　— "The Triangle with Four (or More) Sides"

Thinking of going deep sea fishing? You'll think again after you read *Mysteries of the Deep*, a compilation of the best sea stories from the past 47 years of FATE Magazine. From Atlantis to the Bermuda Triangle, from the Loch Ness Monster to giant jellyfish, you'll find more than a few reasons to stay out of the water. The reports presented here come from the personal experiences of the average citizen as well as the detailed investigations of well-known authors such as Martin Caidin, Dr. Karl P. N. Shuker, Jerome Clark, and Mark Chorvinsky.

Now, from the safety of your beach chair, you can enjoy the best accounts of sea serpents ... lake monsters ... merfolk ... ghost ships ... mysterious shipwrecks ... the search for ancient vessels ... cities under the sea ... and many other ocean oddities.

1-56718-260-7, 256 pp., 5³⁄₁₆ x 8, illus.　　　　　　　　　　**$9.95**

Out of Time and Place

*Amazing Accounts that
Challenge our View of Human History*

Edited by Terry O'Neill

> *I held my hand out of the wagon window and caught four fat,
> brown little toads ... I had heard of fish and frogs falling from the
> clouds, but I had never heard of a fall of toads ...*
> — "Does it Rain Toads?"

Explore fascinating mysteries of history, archaeology, and the paranormal with this collection of amazing reports published only in the pages of FATE magazine. The writers of these fascinating articles follow the footsteps of Indiana Jones, seeking the lost and trying to solve the mysteries of the oddly found. Thirty original articles from the best of FATE over the past 40 years feature tales of lost cities, strange falls from the sky, extraordinary creatures, and misplaced artifacts that call into question our entire view of human history.

Despite studies by historians and scientists from many fields, these events and objects from out of time and place remain unexplained. Readers can't resist being enthralled by these mysteries and by the efforts to solve them.

1-56718-261-5, 272 pp., 5³⁄₁₆ x 8   **$9.95**

Phantom Army of the Civil War

From the files of FATE Magazine

Compiled and Edited by Frank Spaeth

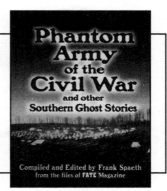

Why did a mysterious apparition of a tall woman draped in white leave a red rose as a token of her visits? Fifty years later, the dried rose remains as evidence of her strange presence ...

Phantom Army of the Civil War features 35 stories of personal encounters with spirits throughout the South, filled with a flavor and tone that is truly and uniquely Southern. From Tennessee to Texas, and Louisiana to Virginia, these tales represent the best Southern ghost stories ever to appear in FATE Magazine during the past forty years. You will meet angry ghosts, still looking for answers as to why they are no longer alive ... phantoms roaming the countryside searching for their lost loves ... grandmothers protecting their kin from beyond the grave ... and many, many more.

1-56718-297-6, 256 pp., 5 ³⁄₁₆ x 8 ¼, softcover   **$9.95**

The Ultimate Alien Agenda

The Re-engineering of Humankind

James L. Walden, Ed.D.

One night, teacher, counselor and public servant Jim Walden was awakened by a red-eyed alien creature at the foot of his bed. He was abducted and subjected to humiliating and painful scientific procedures in a mystifying underground lab. Frightened and on the brink of suicide, he sought the help of a renowned alien-abductee researcher.

Under hypnotic regression, Jim learned that he was an alien-human "hybrid." In this book Jim shares his experiences, discoveries, and his astounding conclusion: that aliens may not be gruesome creatures bent on destroying the human race. Rather, they may be our own ancestors, once revered by ancient human civilizations as reptilian gods. Now they are simply extensions of the human family, and they live in an alternate dimension here on Earth, working to preserve the planet.

- Presents a fascinating first-person account of the creation of an alien-human hybrid
- Provides plausible theories that address eternal questions about the origins of the human race and the evolution of human intelligence
- Offers new perspectives and theories about UFOs and alien encounters, which distinguished investigators have failed to grasp

1-56718-779-X, 320 pp., 5 ³⁄₁₆ x 8, illus.   **$9.95**

UFOs Over Topanga Canyon

*Eyewitness Accounts of the
California Sightings*

Preston Dennett

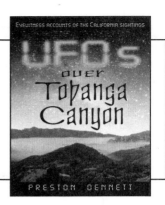

The rural Californian community of Topanga Canyon is home to 8,000 close-knit residents, the Topanga State Park—and an unusual amount of strange activity going on in the sky.

Like Hudson Valley, N.Y., and Gulf Breeze, Fla., Topanga Canyon is considered a UFO hot-spot, with sightings that began more than fifty years ago and continue to this day. Here is the first book to present the activity in the witnesses' own words.

Read new cases of unexplained lights, metallic ships, beams of light, face-to-face alien encounters, UFO healings, strange animal sightings, animal mutilations, and evidence of a government cover-up. There are even six cases involving missing time abductions, and a possible on-board UFO experience.

1-56718-221-6, 312 pp., 5 ³/₁₆ x 8, illus., softcover   **$12.95**

True Hauntings

Spirits with a Purpose

Hazel M. Denning, Ph.D.

Do spirits feel and think? Does death automatically promote them to a paradise—or as some believe, a hell? Real-life ghostbuster Dr. Hazel M. Denning reveals the answers through case histories of the friendly and hostile earthbound spirits she has encountered. Learn the reasons spirits remain entrapped in the vibrational force field of the earth: fear of going to the other side, desire to protect surviving loved ones, and revenge. Dr. Denning also shares fascinating case histories involving spirit possession, psychic attack, mediumship and spirit guides. Find out why spirits haunt us in *True Hauntings,* the only book of its kind written from the perspective of the spirits themselves.

1-56718-218-6, 240 pp., 6 x 9, index, glossary, softcover $12.95

In the Presence of Aliens

*A Personal Experience
of Dual Consciousness*

Janet Bergmark

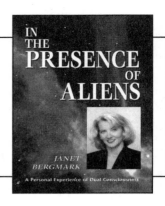

Strange beings remembered from childhood ... ships in the sky over her Wisconsin farm ... the feel of long, bony fingers on her flesh ... and awakening to an alien presence that shares her existence. Science fiction? Not for Janet Bergmark, whose extraordinary, true-life account of the emotional, psychological and spiritual impact of alien contact poignantly captures the rare human experience of coming face-to-face with other sentient beings.

In the Presence of Aliens is the first book to speak candidly about the concept of a dual identity—human and alien; one body, two minds; two minds, one purpose—and its role in explaining why certain people are abducted by nonhuman life forms. Not only does this book explain how a dual identity is possible, it provides a first-person narrative of this unique and sometimes difficult relationship, including actual dialogue between human and alien.

1-56718-063-9, 224 pp., 6 x 9, softcover   **$12.95**

Time Travel

A New Perspective

J.H. Brennan

J. H. BRENNAN

TIME TRAVEL

A NEW PERSPECTIVE

Scattered throughout the world are the skeletal remains of men and women from long before humanity appeared on the planet, and a human footprint contemporary with the dinosaurs. Where did they come from? Are these anomalies the litter left by time travelers from our own distant future? *Time Travel* is an extraordinary trip through some of the most fascinating discoveries of archaeology and physics, indicating that not only is time travel theoretically possible, but that future generations may actually be engaged in it. In fact, the latest findings of physicists show that time travel, at a subatomic level, is already taking place. Unique to this book is the program—based on esoteric techniques and the findings of parapsychology and quantum physics—which enables you to structure your own group investigation into a form of vivid mental time travel.

1-56718-085-X, 224 pp., 6 x 9, photos, softcover   **$12.95**

Poltergeists & The Paranormal

Fact Beyond Fiction

Dr. Philip Stander &
Dr. Paul Schmolling

Poltergeist phenomena make up the most enduring and persuasive body of data concerning the paranormal. The similarities between early and recent cases are quite striking, as are the similarities among cases reported in different parts of the world. Poltergeist events, in turn, support the possibility of psychokinesis—the influence of the mind on physical objects.

Here are the most fascinating cases in the annals of parapsychology—dating from early history to the present. *Poltergeists & the Paranormal* contains never-before-published "evidential cases"—those reported by respected eye witnesses—along with studies conducted by eminent scientists under controlled conditions.

The most up-to-date summary of poltergeist and psychokinetic phenomena available, this book presents a range of possible explanations, permitting you to decide for yourself which theory, explanation or hypothesis is most fitting.

1-56718-682-3, 240 pp., 5 ¼ x 8   **$12.95**